H

...nschild

NY

OK

rkbook

ck, Pop

z Music

D1437779

Volume I

Imprint

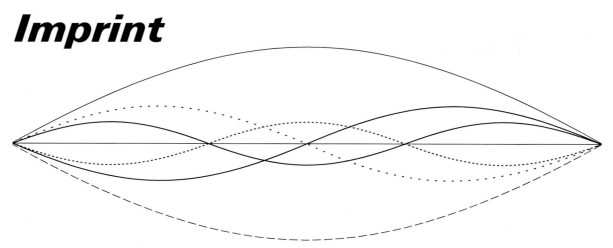

A sine tone and its first two harmonics.

Enlarged and revised new 1994 edition
Copyright © 1988, 1994, 1997 by
AMA Verlag GmbH
Postfach 1168
D-50301 Brühl
Germany

Cover graphics: Manfred Drechsel, Brühl
Photography: Dieter Stork

Desktop publishing: René Teichgräber
Overall production: Detlef Kessler

Printed in Germany

ISBN 3-927190-68-3

Translator's Note

There are some terminological differences in music between American and British English, particularly regarding the names of the notes and rest values. The American term is put first and is followed by the British equivalent using an slash, e.g. "half note/minim". This is not done throughout the entire book as the terms repeat themselves and the reader will quickly become familiar with them. Both the American and the British terms are to be found in the alphabetical index at the end of this book.

Steve Taylor

Contents

Part II:
The Rudiments of Harmony

Chapter 3:

Chapter 4:

Chapter 5:

Four-note chords and their extensions 55

Chapter 6:

The Ionian system 69

Chapter 7:
The circle of fifths

Chapter 8:
The harmonic minor scale

Chapter 9:

Chapter 10:

Chapter 11:

Appendix:

Preface

This book on harmony is meant to be for each and every musician. Irrespective of whether you are an instrumentalist, vocalist, composer, arranger, sound engineer, music teacher or student; the information contained in this textbook is essential for your day-to-day contact with music. It is for this reason that I have endeavoured to make each individual section of this book as detailed and as lucid as possible.

This book is also designed to be used at music schools, colleges and conservatories, where multitudes of classically trained teachers are faced with the problem of having to impart the terminology of rock, pop and jazz music to their eagerly awaiting students. It is here that this book - especially in the legendary and enigmatic field of improvisation - can be an aid both to teaching and learning. It should be used to try to bridge the gap and unite the oft antagonistic camps of classical harmony and popular music by applying their rudiments and relating them to each other.

This harmony method is published in two volumes and is subdivided into different sections, the first two of which will be dealt with in this volume. The tonal system of western harmony is explained in the first part. To enable even the true beginner to learn a little about harmony, the book's first chapter deals with notation. This work thus attempts the virtually impossible: it should, without even calling upon the help of a teacher, serve the layperson as a textbook - even though this may not appear to be worth recommending to most of the experienced educators.

Using the harmonic series, the second chapter illustrates the origins of our tonal system, which are to be found in nature. It can be omitted if the reader wishes to limit him- or herself to learning the rules of harmony. These often neglected facts are, however, of considerable significance for understanding larger interrelationships, which is why I would recommend each reader - perhaps after having read the didactic section - to have a look at this part.

It is the third chapter of the second part of this book which gets down to dealing with the real theory of harmony. The sequence of the chapters has been arranged in such a way that they go from monophony (intervals) right up to the more complex polyphony (triads and chords of four notes). The chords presented are first of all seen as static forms which only later take on the shape of larger-scale harmonic serial forms. There is an introduction in the sixth chapter (Ionian system) to the way of thinking of the modern chord-scale theory, which this harmony method is based on. The chapter on the circle of fifths is followed by all the important and common scales together with the chords based upon them.

There is a whole range of examples for each important subject and they are generally to be found after the paragraph in question. The references printed in *italics* make it easy to find the explanatory text to the individual examples, and in addition, important terms are printed in **bold** type the first time they appear, so that this textbook lends itself to a sort of encyclopaedia or dictionary of harmony for quickly browsing over certain headwords.

There is an alphabetic index of the most important headwords and special terms of harmony at the end, to enable careful, thorough and academic work to be carried out when using this book. You will find a selection of tasks and exercises at the end of each chapter, which will serve to check what you have learnt and which will help you to gain the confidence needed when dealing with such material. The answer key at the end of this book should only really be used in cases of doubt or to check tasks you have already solved.

Many people helped me so much while I was working on this book and I would like to take this opportunity to express my heartfelt gratitude to them. I would mention Detlef Kessler, without whose energy this whole project would never have got off the ground, Michael Küttner, who supported me during my times of trouble with my computer, Eddy Marron, Gunnar Plümer, Herbert Kraus, Denis Wieger and my father Hans-Hilger Haunschild, who all looked through the manuscript critically. I would particularly like to mention Wolfgang Fiedler and René Teichgräber for the page make-up, Manfred Drechsel for the graphic design and Steve Taylor for the English translation. My particularly profound thanks, however, go to my wife Sabine for her constant support and encouragement and to my children Lisa and Felix.

I would refer those who have enjoyed reading the first volume of this work and would like to learn more about harmonic relationships, to the second volume of this book on harmony. It is also published by AMA Verlag and in addition to matters such as II-V-I-progressions, modal changes, tritone substitutes, secondary dominants, turnarounds and the blending of major and minor, it contains a four-colour diatonic modulation table in DIN A1 format. I hope I am able with this book to bring the reader closer to what for me has always been the driving force behind my pre-occupation with harmony, and that is simply the love of music.

Bonn, Autumn 1988

Part I
The Tonal System

Chapter 1
An Introduction to Notation

In order to be able to communicate and explain musical processes between individual musicians we have to agree upon certain signs and symbols. Indeed, there is a whole range of such signs which you should familiarize yourself with. All these contractions and symbols will be listed during the course of this book and their use will be explained. This should not happen, however, until the nature of the subject area makes it necessary.

The most informative, universally applicable and thus, at the same time the most complex, of these systems of symbols is **notation**. Even today, learning notation seems to present many people with quite a few problems, which is why it should be explained right at the beginning of this book so that it loses its terrifying effect. All those who can already read and write music can simply now turn to the next chapter.

The System of Notation

The five-line **system of notation** forms the basis of notation. We do not, for instance, write our notes in little squares or rhombuses; we write them on and between these five lines. Positioning the note fixes the **pitch** and the higher the line the note is on, the higher the note is that then has to be played *(Example 1)*. As long as we are only concerned with the pitch we need do nothing more than depict the notes as open circles.

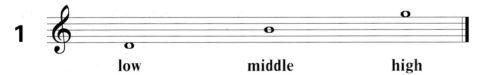

1   low   middle   high

The Clef Question

So as to be able to give names to these notes we first have to avail ourselves of a so-called **clef**. The **treble clef** is by far the most common of these clefs, and it embraces the second line from the bottom with its belly. The treble clef determines that the note called "**g**" is to be on this line *(Example 2)*, and for this reason it is also called the **G clef**.

2

g

f

Another important clef is the **bass clef**, which has the second line from the top between its two dots. It fixes the note on this line as an "**f**", which is why this clef is also called the **F clef** *(Example 2)*. On occasions **alto** and **tenor clefs** are also used (Example 3).

3

c   c

After having decided upon the treble or bass clef — depending on the instrument we would like to play the notes on — we can now incorporate the other notes into the system of notation using the note that has already been fixed. The notes are placed alternately on the lines or in the spaces between the lines, so that, for instance, the note between the second and third line from the bottom is precisely one note higher than the "**g**" fixed by the treble clef *(Example 4)*.

4

g   a

The ABC of Notes

The **alphabet** from "a" to "g" is used to give each note its name (it is perhaps interesting to note that the German system also includes the letter "**h**"). As we have already used the treble and bass clef to fix one note on each of them, it's now easy to give a name to each of the other notes in the sequence according to their pitch *(Examples 5 and 6)*.

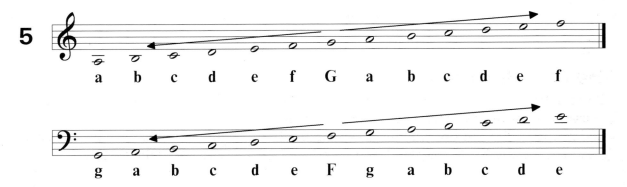

5

a   b   c   d   e   f   G   a   b   c   d   e   f

g   a   b   c   d   e   F   g   a   b   c   d   e

6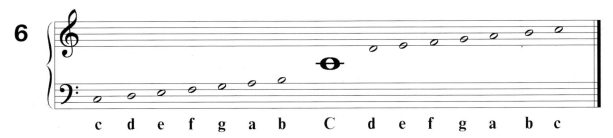

c   d   e   f   g   a   b   C   d   e   f   g   a   b   c

It would seem at this point worth delving into the mysteries of the German note "**h**", if only to satisfy the curiosity of those of you (the translator included) who have always wondered why the note "**b**" is "**h**" in the German-speaking world, thus enabling Bach's name, for instance, to be used as a 4-note musical theme "**B-A-C-H**" (to make things even more complicated the German note "**b**" is "**b** flat"), as in Bach's own "Art of Fugue" (Die Kunst der Fuge) or the slow movement of Beethoven's string quartet op. 59, no. 2 (in the bass). The origin of this enigma can be traced back to a simple slip of the pen of a mediaeval monk who mixed up "**h**" with "**b**". Other monks - ever conscientious as they were - then copied this mistake again and again, and that was that; the note "**h**" spread ever further afield *(Example 7)*.

7

German: **h**   international: **b**

international:

a   b   c   d   e   f   g

We can see then that the notes are named after the first seven letters of the alphabet. Logically enough, the note "**a**" was and is the first note, as evidenced by the fact that most instruments are tuned to the "**concert pitch a**", which was fixed at the internationally recognized **frequency** of **440 Hertz** at the conference on tuning standards in London in 1939.[1]

---

1 New research by Hans Cousto has solved the centuries-old problem of the concert pitch, which was assumed lost. Cousto calculated a concert pitch of **a** = 435.92 Hertz on the basis of his findings that the twenty fourth octave of the frequency of an average solar day corresponds to the note "**g**" (Hans Cousto: *"Die Oktave, das Urgesetz der Harmonie"*, *Verlag Simon und Leutner, Berlin 1987* and *"Klänge, Bilder, Welten - Musik im Einklang mit der Natur"*, *Verlag Simon und Leutner, Berlin 1989*).

Half Tones and Whole Tones

Let's first just have a look at our notes in Examples 5 and 6 again. These notes seem to be spaced at the same distance to each other but this is most certainly not the case, for we must differentiate between **half tones/semitones** and **(whole) tones**. The half tone is the smallest possible distance between two notes in our occidental tonal system. A tone can be divided into two half tones. Two notes which come after one another in steps are generally one tone apart from each other. There are only two exceptions *(Example 8)*: there is always the distance of one half tone between the notes "**e**" and "**f**" and between the notes "**b**" and "**c**". The whole tones are commonly marked with a square bracket and the half tones with a bracket coming to a point .

8   e   f   b   c

The C Major Scale

Armed with this knowledge it is possible to create **the C major scale** *(Example 9)*, which may be regarded as the basis of our entire western tonal system. This C major scale has the following structure: it consists of seven notes, the eighth being the same as the first again, and the half tones are invariably between the third and the fourth and the seventh and the eighth note. Virtually all 7-note (heptatonic) scales are made up of 5 tones and 2 half tones. This specific change of whole-tone and half-tone steps is called **diatonicism**. The C major scale is thus a **diatonic scale**.

= half tone/semitone   = (whole)tone

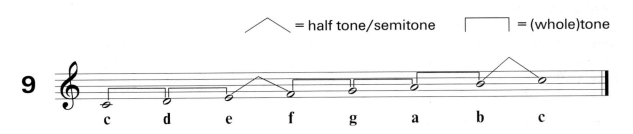

9   c   d   e   f   g   a   b   c

The eighth note of this scale, like the first note, is also called "**c**", from which we may conclude that the names of the other notes repeat themselves as well, as soon as we continue the scale further up or down *(Example 10)*. If we want to write notes which go above or below the 5 lines (staff) we use so-called **ledger lines**, which in turn are the same distance from the upper or lower line as the lines are among themselves.

Accidentals

We can tell from the C major scale in Example 9 that there must be hitherto unknown half tones/semitones between the whole tones of this scale. However, with this scale they cannot be made visible, nor can they be defined using the names of notes we have so far had. It is for this reason that we avail ourselves of so-called **accidentals** to give these notes a name.

Let's start with the **sharp** (♯), which raises the note it stands before by one half tone. The name of the note now simply consists of the original name of the note with the added word "sharp", and becomes, for instance, "f sharp" *(Example 11)*.

It can be useful to raise the pitch of a note by two half tones, and in this case we use a **double sharp,** which looks like an "X". The note is then simply called for instance "f double sharp" *(Example 12)*. For reasons of simplicity though, we seldom make use of this option. It should therefore be examined on a case to case basis whether the enharmonically changed note of the same pitch can't be used instead *(see Page 36, Example 7)*.

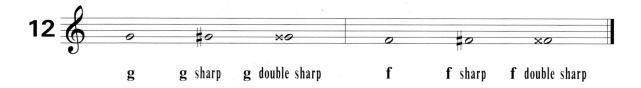

The **flat** accidental (♭) performs the opposite function. It lowers the note it stands before by one half tone and the name of the note now consists of the original name of the note with the added word "flat" and becomes, for instance, "**g flat**". A note lowered by two half tones simply has two flats before it and is called e.g. "**g double flat**" *(Example 13)*.

13

c　　　c flat　　　g　　　g flat　　g double flat　　a　　　a flat

The accidentals remain in force for the duration of one measure/bar only and are cancelled from the next bar line. The effect of the accidental can be neutralized by the **natural sign** (♮), which likewise remains in force only to the next bar line *(Example 14)*.

14

f sharp　　f sharp　　　f　　　f sharp　　　f sharp　　　f

If, however, the accidentals are to retain their effect for the duration of the whole piece, they are placed at the beginning of the score *(Example 15)*. This group of sharps or flats is known as the **key signature** *(see Page 84, Examples 11 and 12)*.

15

f sharp　　　　c sharp　　　　f sharp　　　　c sharp

The Twelve Notes within an Octave

If we want to close the gaps between the tones of a major scale with the half tones between them we can do this with the aid of the accidentals mentioned above, and this can best be illustrated with a piano keyboard. The white keys are the notes of the C major scale and the black keys are the half tones between them *(Example 16)*.

16

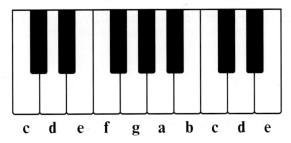

c　d　e　f　g　a　b　c　d　e

If we decide to use sharps to name the notes that fall on these black keys then we have **c sharp, d sharp, f sharp, g sharp** and **a sharp** *(Example 17)*.

In this case we have raised the corresponding notes on the white piano keys by a half tone. If we wish to employ flat accidentals we have to lower the notes above them, in which case they are then called **d flat, e flat, g flat, a flat** and **b flat** *(Example 18)*.

The sequence of all twelve half tones within one octave is called a **chromatic scale** *(Example 19)*. The term **chromatic** finds its origins in Greek (khrõma = colour) and is best translated with "semitonality".

Four-Four Time

Now that we are able to order the notes according to their pitch and to give them a name, it's time to incorporate the **sound duration** into the notation. However, we first have to fix the length of a **measure/bar**. A bar is the smallest unit in the splitting up of a piece of music into rhythm and time and it is marked using **bar lines**. A time signature you frequently come across is the **four-four time** or **common time**, and as the name reveals already, it contains four quarter notes/crotchets *(see Example 22)*.

The Time Values of Notes

Our presentation of the various note lengths begins with the **whole note/semibreve**, which takes the form of an open circle and completely fills up a four-four measure. This is made evident by the next bar line *(Example 20)*.

This whole note can be divided up into two **half notes/minims**, which, in contrast to whole notes, are given a stem *(Example 21)*.

These note stems are written upwards up to and including the note "**a**" and downwards from the note "**b**" (which is exactly in the middle of the staff). The half notes/minims can in turn be subdivided into two **quarter notes/crotchets**, which have their **note head** filled in *(Example 22)*. These quarter notes/crotchets may be seen as the basic pulse for the rhythm and as the unit for counting a measure/bar, and it is for this reason that they are often referred to as **beats** (e.g. "The whole note lasts for 4 beats").

If we want to split these quarter notes up even further we have to add **tails** to the stems. There is one tail with **eighth notes/quavers**, two with **sixteenth notes/semiquavers**, three with **thirty-second notes/demisemiquavers** and so on *(Example 23)*.

If there are several consecutive notes with a tail they are joined up using a beam *(Example 24)*.

Triplets

If the note value is to be split up into values other than the dividing into two mentioned above, then **triplets** are the answer. This entails joining up 3 notes of the next smallest rhythmic type into one unit. With **quarter-note/crotchet triplets** we use a square bracket and with **eighth-note/quaver triplets** a rounded bracket *(Example 25)*. The duration of a quarter-note triplet is thus the value of a half note and that of the eighth-note triplet a quarter note. We can see then that the half or the quarter notes are each divided up into three notes of equal length.

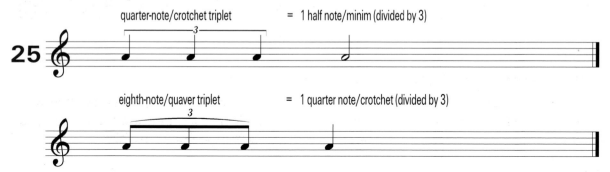

Rest Signs

The next thing we should have a look at and commit to memory is **rest signs,** whose values correspond exactly to the note values we have already discussed *(Example 26)*. In this example the whole-note/semibreve rest is followed by the half-note/minim rest, then the **quarter-note/crotchet rest**, the **eighth-note/quaver rest** and the **sixteenth-note/semiquaver rest**.

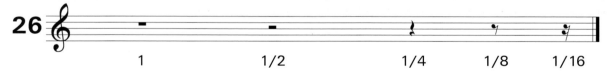

Dots and Ties

In connection with note and rest values there are two more special features which make writing rhythmic division easier. A **dot** placed after a note or a rest enables intermediate values to be fixed. This dot increases the note or rest by exactly half of its original value. Let's take a look at the example of a half note, which has two beats (a beat can basically be regarded as equivalent to a quarter note). If we now put a dot after this half note it increases the length by half of its value and thus lasts three beats *(Example 27)*.

The same goes of course for eighth and sixteenth notes or rests. The **tie** enables notes to be lengthened beyond the bar line *(Example 28)*.

Other Time Signatures (Metres)

Now that we have familiarized ourselves with the note values and rest signs within 4/4 time it is possible to change the metre, which generally means that the bars take on a different length. A simple example illustrating this is **3/4 time** *(Example 29)*.

We see here that the next bar line is placed after *three* quarter notes. There are of course other important time signatures such as 5/4, 6/4 or 12/8 and many others.

The scope of this book does not allow detailed treatment of this subject, and in any case the knowledge already gained about notes, note values, rests and time signatures is more than enough for an understanding of harmonic relationships.

Expression Marks

There are many more abbreviations and expression marks which are found in notation and I would recommend that the reader consult a general book on music or a music encyclopaedia or dictionary of music as the need arises: the multitude of terms would stretch this book way beyond its limits. These expression marks in any case have little relevance for harmony as they refer only to the way the music should be interpreted.

Chapter 1 Exercises

1. What are the following notes called (fill in the names)?

a.

g

b.

2. What are the values of the following notes?

1/1

3. Supply the missing notes.

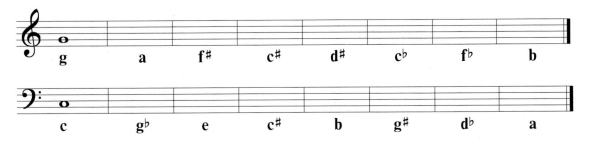

g   a   f#   c#   d#   cᵇ   fᵇ   b

c   gᵇ   e   c#   b   g#   dᵇ   a

4. Complete the bars with the correct note values.

1/4

5. Complete the bars with the correct rest values.

1/2

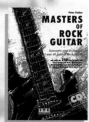

Chapter 2

The Phenomenon of the Harmonic Series - The Basis of Harmony

If you pluck a string on any stringed instrument and make it sound you may well detect not only the **fundamental tone**, which sounds the loudest, but also a whole range of **harmonics** or **overtones**, as they are also called. They generally come across though, as **tone colour**. The sum total of these sounds - fundamental tone and overtones - thus form together the tonal characteristic of this note. The overtones are present in the sound of each and every natural source of sound and largely shape the tonal colour of the instrument or sound generator. There are countless numbers of these overtones but as far as our tonal system and this theory of harmony are concerned it is only the first 15 harmonics that are relevant. If we add the fundamental tone to the 15 overtones you get a series of 16 tones which are termed the "**partial tone series**" *(Example 1)*.

The Octave Positions

The fundamental tone "C" in this example is, therefore, the first partial of this partial tone series; the first overtone or harmonic "c" may then be regarded as the second partial of this partial tone series. These two sounds with the same name are one **octave** apart from each other, which means that their vibrations per second are in a proportion of 1:2 to each other. The vibrations of a tone per second are called "**Hertz**" after the German physicist Heinrich Hertz. The fundamental tone "C" of the partial tone series illustrated above has a **frequency** of 64 Hertz, meaning that it vibrates up and down in the air 64 times in one second. The first harmonic (also called upper partial) is one octave higher and has a frequency of 128 Hertz.

In order to make a clearer distinction between these notes with the same name, which are one or several octaves apart from each other, the **octave positions** have been termed differently. The contraoctave starts with C', which has 32 Hertz. There then follows the great octave, which begins with the fundamental tone of our partial tone series (C), and after this the small octave (c), the one-line octave (c'), the two-line octave (c'') and the three-line octave (c''') *(Example 2)*.The great and the small octaves are in the bass clef while the one- and two-line octaves are written in the treble clef.

The Octave Positions

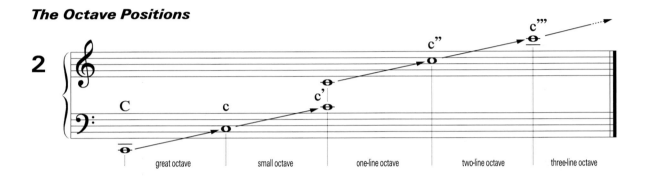

Frequency Ratios and Interval Proportions

The ratio of the vibrations of the harmonic series' individual tones to each other springs constant surprises upon us, and it is the partial's number that reveals its frequency ratio to the fundamental tone. We have already seen that the second partial has a ratio of 2:1 to the fundamental tone i.e. it has double the frequency of the fundamental tone. The third partial accordingly has triple the frequency of the fundamental tone, and in our example with "C" as the fundamental tone this is then 192 Hertz. It therefore follows that each subsequent tone has the same constant spacing to the previous one of 64 Hertz.

The following graph demonstrates the ratio of the harmonic series to the corresponding frequency values. There are 16 partials on the horizontal axis and the corresponding frequency values on the vertical axis. The straight line shows the function of the frequencies in relation to the partials. If you get a straight line in such a functional diagram it is a so-called linear function. The relationship of the partials to their frequency values is thus a linear function *(Example 3)*.

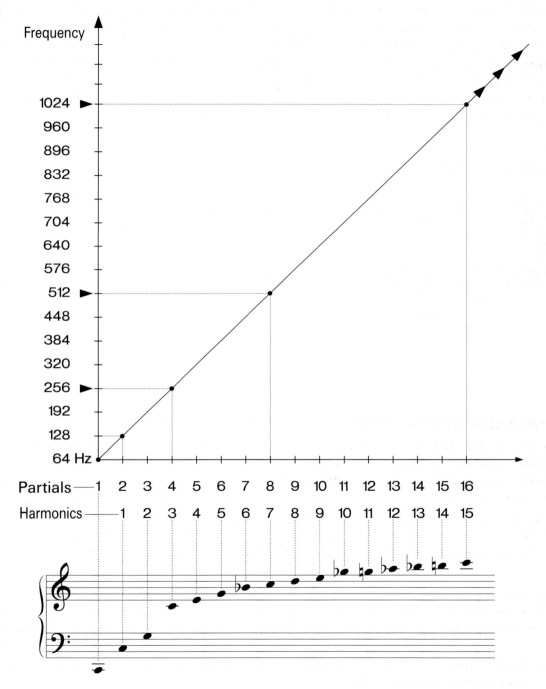

3

The number of a partial also discloses the point on a string which you must divide by laying your finger on it, and which will then produce the corresponding tones of the harmonic series. The monochord, an ancient musical instrument with only one string, served the Greeks as an object to demonstrate this division ratio. The string has to be divided exactly in the middle to sound the first harmonic, the octave. The tone played is thus in a ratio of 2:1 to the open string. The octave is the second partial and can make do with half the string length. The third partial needs only one third of the string length, the next one only a quarter and so on, right up to the three-line c, which manages with just one sixteenth of the string length.

It turns out that the division ratio of the string is inversely proportional to the frequency. If, for instance, you stop a third of the string and pluck the other two thirds (2:3), the fifth of the fundamental tone sounds, which has one-and-a-half times the frequency of the fundamental tone (1.5:1). Or if we stop a quarter of the string and let three quarters vibrate freely (3:4) the fourth sounds, whose frequency has a ratio of 1.33333:1 to the fundamental note. The division ratios of a string for fixing the intervals are called **interval proportions** *(see also Page 40, Example 13).*

The harmonic series is really the "natural" scale of all music and for this reason is occasionally called the **natural harmonic series**. The harmonic series in Example 1 would be produced if you blew a valveless horn tuned to C or if you took any stringed instrument and generated the harmonics on a string tuned to C. These are tones produced by gently placing a finger on an exact point (e.g. a half, a third, a quarter or a fifth of the string length). With a guitar, for instance, you can get the first five of these harmonics one after the other on the 12th, 7th, 5th, 4th and 3rd fret. It's even easier with an electric bass guitar with round wound strings; you just need to try a few times and you will soon be able to hear nearly all 15 of the harmonics.

The Well-Tempered Tuning

It goes without saying that the intervals between the individual overtones get smaller and smaller the higher we go in the partial tone series. The frequency spacing, however, remains constant and this leads to degrees in the upper area of the harmonic series which do not appear in today's music and which may therefore seem to be of no use. They cannot even be notated accurately with the system of notation we have. Through the extension of the tonal area and through **modulations**, i.e. the relationship of intervals and chords to several fundamental tones, impurities in the sound are produced if the harmonic series from one fundamental tone is used as a basis, and it is because of this that the necessity for a balanced **well-tempered tuning** becomes all too evident. This is done by dividing the octave into 12 equal half tones so that only the octave with the vibration ratio of 1:2 is pure or perfect.

This well-tempered tuning, which was first introduced to the Western world by Andreas Werckmeister in 1691, has primarily become known through "Das Wohltemperierte Clavier" by Johann Sebastian Bach. Bach demonstrated the practicality of this tuning by composing a prelude and a fugue in each key. Through **enharmonic change** this well-tempered tuning treats all the chromatic notes as equal *(see Page 36, Example 7)* and today it applies to every instrument. This tuning is a kind of compromise: the octave is divided up into twelve equal intervals even though this means that all the intervals (except the octave itself) no longer correspond to the "perfect" original intervals from the harmonic series. As a result, tracing back certain musical facts to the origin of the harmonic series is made more difficult because many frequencies and interval proportions - due to this well-tempered tuning - no longer quite correspond to the "natural" tones.

There are still many secrets hidden away in the harmonic series and its structure. The entire rudiments of harmony such as intervals, triads or scales as well, can be derived from the number ratios of the overtones. These relationships will be referred to at the proper time during the course of the next chapter, but one thing that has now already been established is the fact that musical feeling is very closely connected to simple physical and mathematical circumstances, and that relatively simple laws can therefore be found - just as is the case with the two sciences mentioned - which can serve as the basis for the entire structure of musical expression.

Chapter 2 Exercises

1. Try writing down the harmonic series using a different fundamental tone ("perhaps with "**D**"), which shouldn't be too difficult if you look at the model given *(Example 1).*

2. Fill in the names of the notes and the corresponding octaves they belong to.

a.

d"

b.

d

3. Fill in the missing notes.

a'   d   f#"   b♭'   G   c   g#'   e"

Part II

The Rudiments of Harmony

Chapter 3
The Intervals

The word **interval** is derived from the Latin word "intervallum" and literally translated actually means "the space between two palisades or ramparts". In music this word stands for the **distance** between two notes. The names of the intervals have come about by simply counting the degrees of a major scale. This system has actually been around since the Middle Ages, which is why the terms are Latin based. The first note of the scale was thus called "primus" or first degree, the second was "secundus" or second degree, followed by "tertius"/third degree, "quartus"/fourth degree, "quintus"/fifth degree etc. *(Example 1).*

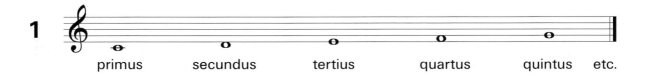

The Perfect Intervals

Let's first take a look at the so-called **perfect intervals**, which are derived direct from the first four tones of the partial tone series. They are the unison, the octave, the fifth and the fourth. The perfect unison is the interval that is between two notes of exactly the same pitch *(Example 2)*. The perfect unison thus describes the absence of any interval between two equal notes. In order to derive the intervals from the harmonic series it is best in this case to enlist the aid of the fundamental tone of the harmonic series.

The interval of the octave - as was seen in Chapter 2 - is between the fundamental tone and the first overtone of the harmonic series; in other words between the first and second partial *(see Page 25, Example 1)*. The interval of the perfect fifth is between the 2nd and the 3rd tone and the perfect fourth between the 3rd and the 4th tone of the partial tone series *(Example 3)*.

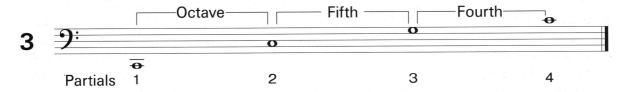

The C major scale provides a very good example of the **perfect intervals** *(Example 4)*. There is a distance of one octave between **c** and **c'**. The perfect fifth may be found not only between **c** and **g** but between **d** and **a** and **e** and **b** as well. And the interval of the perfect fourth is between **c**, **f**, **d** and **g**, **e** and **a**, as well as between **g** and **c'**.

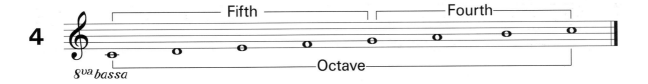

Major and Minor - Diminished and Augmented

Let's now turn our attention to the other intervals in the scale. We have to subdivide all the other intervals into **major** and **minor** in order to describe them more precisely. This then applies to the seconds, the thirds, the sixths and the sevenths. If the unisons, the fourths, the fifths or the octaves are raised or lowered by a half tone they are called **augmented** or **diminished** intervals.

Being the smallest distance between two notes, the half tone may be regarded as the unit for measuring the distance of and determining intervals. There is no distance between the two notes of a unison and it therefore has 0 half tones. An octave has 12 half tones, a fifth 7 and a fourth 5. All the intervals, their names and half tone distances are illustrated in the following table of intervals *(Example 5)*.

Table of Intervals

5

Interval	Name	Half Tones/ Semitones
c - c	(perfect) unison	0
c - d♭	minor second	1
c - d	major second	2
c - d♯	augmented second	3
c - e♭	minor third	3
c - e	major third	4
c - f	(perfect) fourth	5
c - f♯	augmented fourth	6
c - g♭	diminished fifth	6
c - g	(perfect) fifth	7
c - g♯	augmented fifth	8
c - a♭	minor sixth	8
c - a	major sixth	9
c - b♭	minor seventh	10
c - b	major seventh	11
c - c'	(perfect) octave	12

Let's follow the sequence in this table and start with the minor second, which we have already met as the half tone. As I mentioned before, it comes in the C major scale between the notes **e** and **f** and **b** and **c'** *(see Page 15, Examples 8 and 9)*. The interval of a major second, which is often called a (whole) tone, is between the notes **c** and **d**, **d** and **e**, **f** and **g**, **g** and **a** and **a** and **b**. It simply won't do to call such an interval a "second". Just as we have to differentiate between half tones and tones, we also have to distinguish between minor and major seconds. "Minor" and "major" should be seen as an integral part of each and every name of an interval.

There are three half tones in the minor third and it is indeed the first third of a **minor triad** *(see Page 43, Example 3)*. In the C major scale the minor third comes between the notes **d** and **f**, **e** and **g** and **a** and **c'**. The major third is made up of four half tones and can be found in the C major scale *(see Example 4)* between **c** and **e**, **f** and **a** and **g** and **b**. The minor sixth (8 half tones) is located between **e** and **c'**, the major sixth (9 half tones) between **c** and **a** and **d** and **b**. The interval of the minor seventh (10 half tones) is between **d** and **c'** and to round it off we have the major seventh (11 half tones) which is between the notes **c** and **b**.

It is easy to see from this table that it is not possible to get by with just the perfect, the minor and the major intervals, and that the diminished and the augmented intervals do have to be added in order to be able to define precisely every conceivable interval between two notes. A diminished interval is one half tone smaller than the minor or perfect interval of the same name. Augmented intervals are correspondingly one half tone bigger.

The Tritone

As the fourth and the fifth are both perfect intervals it is not possible using the present terminology to give a name to the interval that is exactly between the fourth and the fifth. The interval between "**c**" and "**f**♯" should then be regarded as an augmented fourth and the interval between "**c**" and "**g**♭" as a diminished fifth *(Example 6)*.

In both cases the distance is 6 half tones and it is only in the way we write it that there is a difference between the two intervals. These two intervals are generally called **tritone**, which in Latin more or less translates as "three tone", and what is meant here of course - referring to the interval between the two notes - is whole tones (3 whole tones = 6 half tones). It is not, however, exclusively because of its name that the tritone occupies a special position among the intervals *(see page 38, Example 12 and Page 40, Example 13)*.

The Use of Enharmonic Notes

It should be reiterated at this point that the advent of the well-tempered tuning brought with it the **use of enharmonic notes**, which means that all the degrees which result from the note being lowered or raised may be treated as equivalent to differently termed degrees of the same pitch. The consequence of this is that tones with the same sound can be notated and named differently by, for instance, exchanging names of notes with ♯ and ♭. To a certain extent they are indeed exchangeable. This process is known as **enharmonic change**.

A flattened "**c**" (**c**♭) for instance, may just as equally be treated as equivalent to a "**b**", as were the notes "**f**♯" and "**g**♭" mentioned above, or for that matter the notes "**f**♭" and "**e**" *(Example 7)*. The most common enharmonically-related notes have been cited in this example. Despite the range of possibilities through enharmonic change, you should, however, try to stick to using either sharp or flat accidentals when writing music as otherwise the pattern made by a group or page of notes will become too confusing and illegible.

7

The use of enharmonic notes also has an effect on the terms used to describe the intervals. In classical harmony every conceivable interval has a precise name and is clearly defined. I would refer you to the complete list of all the intervals *(Example 8)* to elucidate this point.

8
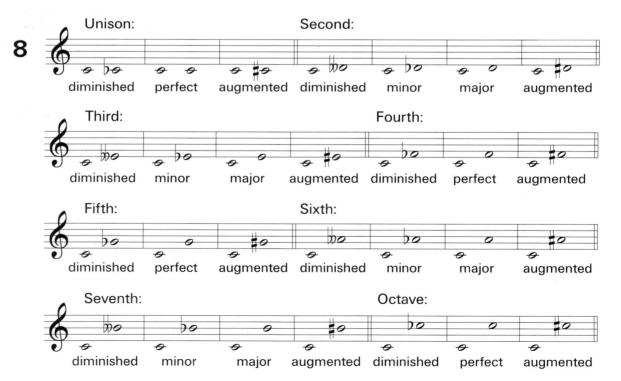

Today, however, attempts are being made to cut back the ever-growing number of special musical terms to a reasonable level, and I would therefore recommend readers to use the somewhat simplified table of intervals *(Page 34, Example 5)* as a working basis because I do feel that it is more than adequate for the requirements of modern harmony.

Beyond the Octave

Intervals going beyond the octave are given their own name. We can, if we want, just make do with first forming an octave from the lower note of the interval and then measuring the remaining distance from the octave of the fundamental tone *(Example 9)*.

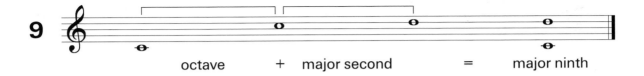

This may well be quite a good way of determining the distance but the term "octave plus major second", used in our example to describe the interval, is somewhat awkward and not exactly elegant. It is most important that these intervals be termed correctly, particularly as they will later be used with chord symbols, and in any case they progress logically and are therefore easy to remember. They are simply called: ninth, tenth, eleventh, twelfth and thirteenth *(Example 10)*.

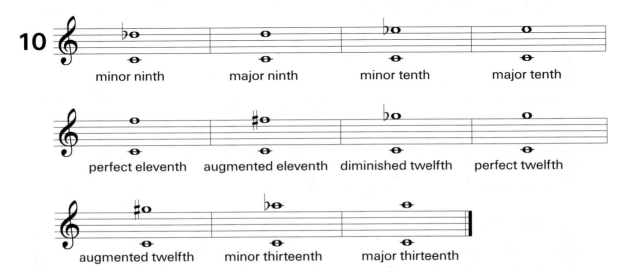

Complementary Intervals

Intervals which complement each other forming one octave are called **complementary intervals**. They are very closely related to one another and demonstrate a similar degree of consonance or dissonance, a subject which will be gone into in the next section. In order to be able to form the complementary interval into an already fixed interval we simply transpose the lower one of the two tones an octave higher *(Example 11)*.

11

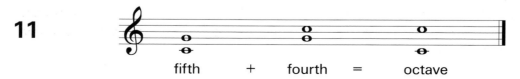

fifth   +   fourth   =   octave

What this actually means then is doubling any frequency (to reach the next higher octave) or halving it (to reach the next lower octave). The original interval then complements its inverted interval. A complete list of these complementary intervals will certainly not go amiss at this stage *(Example 12)*.

12

unison	–	octave
minor second	–	major seventh
major second	–	minor seventh
minor third	–	major sixth
major third	–	minor sixth
fourth	–	fifth
tritone	–	tritone

The tritone occupies a special position in this respect as well, being the only interval that inverts itself and as a result complements itself. The tritone thus divides the octave into two equal halves.

A Few Observations on Ear Training

We have now more or less reached the end of this chapter on intervals, but to complete the picture I would like to make a few observations on the sadly too often neglected area of **aural or ear training**. The impatient reader - after having done the exercises on intervals - can now go straight on to the next chapter and, should he so wish, come back to the practical aspect of listening to intervals at a later point in time.

Consonance and Dissonance

In addition to the question of just measuring the distance between two tones there is also the matter of a certain **interval quality**. In the main, this quality focuses on the so-called **consonance principle**, which has, however, been subject to violent fluctuations throughout the history of music.

A sign of **consonance** may be regarded as a "high degree of blending" of the two tones, producing an effect of calmness and relaxation. **Dissonance**, on the other hand, leaves an impression of a clash and shrillness and yearning for resolution in a consonance. Seen like this, we could translate consonant with "euphonious" or "pleasant sounding" and dissonant with "full of tension".

Theories of Aural Psychology

Aural psychology divides consonance into three basic theories:

1. The **Theory of Proportions** (after Pythagoras): "The simpler the vibration ratio of two tones to each other is, the more consonant is their interval".

2. The **Theory of Harmonic Relationship** (after Helmholtz): "There will be consonance between two tones if one or several tones of their harmonic series coincide." This is only true, however, for the first 8 upper partials with the exception of the seventh.

3. The **Theory of the Amalgamation of Sound** (after Stumpf): "Two tones are more consonant the more they are felt to be one single tone by untrained listeners". This, however, would be more a difference of quantity than quality.

There are various contexts in harmony in which differentiating certain qualities in intervals is beneficial, for instance when assessing the content of consonance or dissonance of harmonies or melodies. These differences become particularly apparent when dealing with two-part melodies, and even more so when they are contrapuntal.

Ear training provides a further opportunity to use this knowledge of interval qualities in practice. It hardly needs stating that the benefits of a sound, theoretical knowledge will not be reaped until the commensurate aural faculties are at hand. This is why it is essential that what has been learnt in theory should also be consciously heard and listened to. This goes not only for the harmonic series and the intervals but for the triads, chords and scales as well, which will be dealt with in the following chapters.

The Interval Proportions

The Pythagoras' theory of proportions is perhaps the simplest way of ordering the intervals according to sonorous considerations. It can likewise be derived directly from the harmonic series. The following rule applies in this case: the lower the number ratios are, the more consonant the interval is. These ratios of the intervals are now listed in order of their consonance *(Example 13)*.

13

Unison	1:1
Octave	1:2
Fifth	2:3
Fourth	3:4
Major sixth	3:5
Major third	4:5
Minor third	5:6
Minor sixth	5:8
Minor seventh	5:9
Major second	8:9
Major seventh	8:15
Minor second	15:16
Tritone	32:45

The numbers of these **interval proportions** correspond precisely to the numbers of the tones of the partial tone series, which are exactly at the distance described from each other *(see Page 25, Example 1)*. There is for instance the interval of a major sixth between the 3rd and 5th partial (interval proportion 3:5). The one exception (as always) is the tritone, with its ratio of 32:45 not appearing in the harmonic series.

Interval Qualities in Classical Counterpoint

There are also other ways, some of which are much more modern, of classifying intervals in certain categories. I shall but present them one by one here without attempting to assess them. The reader may - depending on his aural faculties, which will develop the more he concerns himself with this subject - choose himself which categorization seems to make the most sense. Each person may well find his own system, but what is important here is first and foremost being able to tell the intervals apart with a certain degree of accuracy after having practised for some time. Since the era of classical counterpoint (16th century) the intervals have been divided up into the following groups *(Example 14)*.

14
> 1. Perfect concords: unison, octave, fifth and fourth with the main note above.
> 2. Imperfect concords: minor and major thirds and sixths.
> 3. Discords: all seconds and sevenths, the fourth with the main tone below and all augmented and diminished intervals.

What is noticeable here is the large degree of concurrence with the Pythagorean theory of proportions even though the fourth is treated differently depending on whether the fundamental tone (of the key of the melody) is above or below.

The Intervals in Jazz

Recent times, especially in the field of jazz, have seen further ways of dividing up the intervals into groups which may be described as more or less consonant or dissonant. They are subdivisions which have come about through composition and arranging practice in jazz, rock and pop. Such a categorization might look like this *(Example 15)*:

15
> 1. Primary concords: major and minor thirds, major and minor sixths.
> 2. Secondary concords: unison, octave and fifth.
> 3. Mild discords: augmented second, augmented fifth, tritone, minor seventh, major second.
> 4. Discords: minor second, major seventh, minor ninth.
> 5. The fourth (which can differ in its effect and is therefore listed separately).

This comparison makes it abundantly clear that there have been several changes since the 16th century. We see that with the consonant intervals, the perfect intervals of the unison, octave, fifth and fourth have virtually changed places with the thirds and the sixths, as far as their degree of consonance is concerned. There is a greater distinction between the discords, with intervals having a so-called **half-tone clash** (the minor second, its complementary interval of the major seventh, and the minor ninth) being the only ones that are regarded as truly dissonant. The remaining intervals are termed "mild discords". What is also noticeable among all these differences, however, is that the fourth is judged in both cases as having characteristics which can produce different effects. We may generally conclude that human appreciation of consonance and dissonance is shifting more and more in favour of dissonance, which in turn means that in this present age an increasing number of intervals and chords which almost certainly used to be classified as discords are now being seen as consonant.

Circles of Intervals

Interval circles are circles around which notes are written clockwise and these notes always have the same interval distance to each other. Apart from the best-known circles of intervals, the **circle of fifths** and the **circle of fourths** *(Vol. I, Page 79 ff.)*, there are more circles of intervals which in certain contexts can be of use *(Vol. I, Page 49 ff. and Vol. II, Page 140 ff.)*.

Chapter 3 Exercises

1a: What are the names of the following intervals?

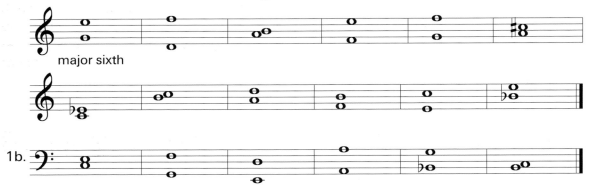

2. Find and name the complementary intervals for these intervals.

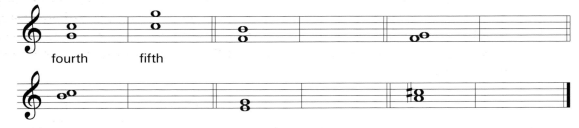

3. How can the following intervals be enharmonically changed and written?

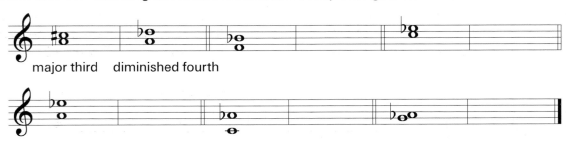

Chapter 4

The Triads

Now that we have dealt with the relationship of two notes to each other, as they appear in monophony with two consecutive notes, we can turn our attention to polyphony and the resultant vertical sound formations or structures which we call **chords**. The simplest chord is the **triad** (also called the **common chord**) and, as its name implies, it consists of three notes. By definition these three notes must be at intervals of a third to each other, or to put it another way: if you put three notes on top of each other in thirds, you have formed a triad. The pattern formed by such a group of three notes can easily be recognized by its "tower-like" shape *(Example 1)*. But as there are both major and minor thirds we can form a total of four different kinds of triads.

1

The Four "Basic" Triads

Let's begin with the **major triad**, which if we start with its **root** (or fundamental tone) first of all has a major third and then a minor third. Both thirds together form an interval of a fifth. The three notes of a major triad correspond to the first six tones of the partial tone series *(see page 25, Example 1)*. A major triad thus consists of its root, the major third and the fifth *(Example 2)*.

2

The opposite is true for the **minor triad**, which first has the minor third and then the major third, consisting therefore of the root, the minor third and the major third. The overall interval remains the fifth and is thus the same with major and minor *(Example 3)*.

3

The **diminished triad** is made up of two minor thirds and its overall interval is a tritone (or a diminished fifth), whilst the **augmented triad** is formed with two major thirds and the overall interval is an augmented fifth *(Example 4)*. Both these triads are thus named after their overall intervals.

Triad Inversions

Any of the notes of the triad can be **doubled at the octave** or they can be played one after the other without losing their identity as a triad *(Example 5)*.

The notes of the triad keep their specific quality as root, third and fifth even if their sequence is inverted. The lowest note determines the type of **inversion**. You invert a triad by raising the lowest note by one octave. We have already seen that the root is at the bottom in the **fundamental root position**, but with the **first inversion** the third is now at the bottom with the fifth of the triad a third higher and the root a sixth higher. This has led to the first inversion also being called **the chord of the $\frac{6}{3}$, the chord of the sixth** or **sixth chord** *(Example 6)*.

With the second inversion we now find the fifth of the triad at the bottom, the root a fourth above and the third a sixth above; the second inversion is accordingly termed the **chord of the $\frac{6}{4}$** *(Example 7)*. We find this $\frac{6}{4}$ chord in the partial tone series from the 3rd to the 5th tone *(see Page 25, Example 1)*.

These inversions are in the main only found with major and minor triads. If you try to invert an augmented triad you simply get another augmented triad with the root a major third higher than that of the original triad. The fact is, then, that an augmented triad inverts itself *(Example 8)*.

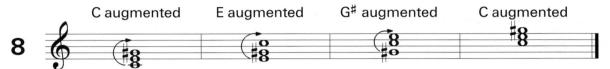

There is not that much difference in sound between the **root position** and the two inversions of the diminished triad, which is why we can forgo distinguishing between them at great lengths *(Example 9)*.

The First Chord Symbols

Chord symbols are used in long passages to avoid having to write every single note of all the triads. They consist mainly of a capital letter with added or superscript letters, numbers or symbols. A major triad, for instance, is defined using the capital letter of its root *(Example 10)*. The capital "**C**" thus denotes a C major triad with the notes **c**, **e** and **g**. If a small "**m**" is now added to the capital letter the corresponding minor triad is meant *(Example 11)*.

Diminished triads have a superscript "zero" added and augmented triads a "plus" sign *(Example 12)*. So we see that such a chord symbol denotes three tones which, depending on what is added or not added to the triad symbol, are put together in major and minor thirds.

AMA
VERLAG

The Diatonic Triads of a Major Scale

If we construct a triad on the root of a major scale, using the notes of that scale, we automatically get a major triad. This procedure can also be applied to the other notes of the scale, thereby enabling a triad to be formed on each note of a major scale *(Example 13)*.

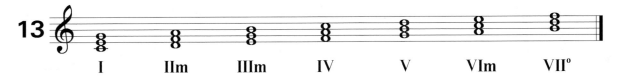

I   IIm   IIIm   IV   V   VIm   VII°

Each degree is described with the aid of the Roman numerals from I to VII and they are used in **functional harmony** starting from the tonic of the key given to show clearly the **degree** of the chord. Such chords are called **diatonic chords**. This being the case, an A minor chord (= Am) can be named VIm, which means nothing more than this Am chord is on the sixth degree in the key of C major.

Primary and Secondary Triads

In classical harmony the 3 major triads on the degrees of the scale I, IV and V are called the **primary triads**. The minor triads on II, III and VI are the **secondary triads**. Few allowances, if any, are made for the diminished triad on VII, with attempts being made to categorize it as a "shortened" dominant seventh chord (without the root) *(see Page 65, Example 21)*.

The Classical Terms of Harmonic Function

It was in 1722 that the 3 primary chords in classical harmony were given certain **terms of harmonic function** by the French composer and theoretician Jean Philippe Rameau (1683 - 1764). Since that time the chord on degree I has been known as the **tonic (T)**, the chord on degree V as the **dominant (D)** and the chord on degree VI as the **subdominant (S)**. These 3 primary chords are **related in fifths** to each other, which means they are at intervals of a fifth and are related to each other via the common origin from the major scale *(Example 14)*.

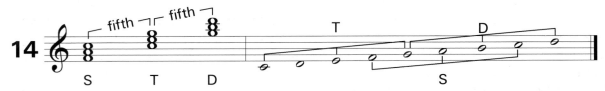

The three secondary triads are **related in thirds** to the primary chords. A **related** or **parallel** minor chord is assigned to each major triad. VI is the **tonic parallel** or **submediant** of I, the chord on III is called the **dominant parallel** or **mediant** and that on II the **subdominant parallel** or **supertonic** *(Example 15)*.

T = tonic	**D** = dominant	**S** = subdominant
Tp = tonic parallel	**Dp** = dominant parallel	**Sp** = subdominant parallel

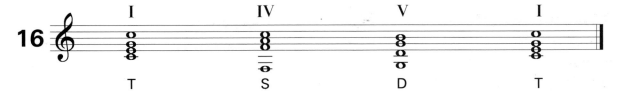

The Fifth Relationship

Since the advent of the major-minor system in the 17th century the **fifth relationship** has been the most frequently occurring relationship between two chords. This becomes clear too, upon closer examination of the **classical cadence**, which serves to establish a particular key and which is formed on the formula I-IV-V-I (for the degrees) or **T-S-D-T** (for the terms of harmonic function) *(Example 16)*. A **cadence** may be defined as a sequence of chords with a logical linking of the individual harmonies and resolution in a final chord.

Functions and Cadences

The three "fifth-related" primary chords fulfil certain functions in the harmonic context and this is easily apparent just by listening to them. The tonic has a certain **finality** to it and is regarded as a resting-point, which is why many compositions begin and end with the major triad on I. The dominant emanates tension or suspense which is generally resolved directly in the tonic. It is primarily the tritone between the major third and the minor seventh of the **dominant seventh chord** that creates this suspense. But this triad on V does have a part to play as a dominant as well. The resolution of a dominant into its tonic is called a **perfect cadence** or an **authentic cadence** *(Example 17)*.

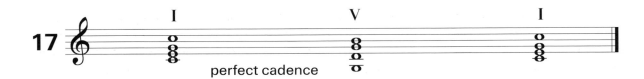

perfect cadence

The subdominant is seen as the **opposite pole** of the tonic, but it too can resolve directly onto the tonic. Resolving the subdominant into its tonic is called a **plagal cadence** *(Example 18)*, and in recent times it has also been christened **gospel cadence** (or Amen cadence) due to it frequently occurring in gospel music.

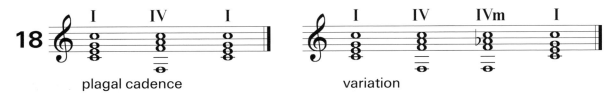

plagal cadence   variation

All endings on the tonic are termed a **full close**, the perfect or authentic and the plagal cadences thus belonging to this category. A sequence of chords ending on the dominant is called an **imperfect cadence**, a **half close** or a **half cadence**. If the tonic does not appear as the expected final chord it is known as an **interrupted, deceptive, abrupt, avoided, broken** or **evaded cadence**, the first two being the most common terms for it. In classical harmony this is generally the dominant followed by the tonic parallel *(Example 19)*.

19

Assigning the Diatonic Triads to the 3 Functional Areas

Not only the primary chords on the degrees I, IV and V can be assigned to the three functional areas of the tonic, the subdominant and the dominant. It is, indeed, all the diatonic triads of a major scale that can assigned to one of these three areas. The chords of the third (III) and sixth degree (VI) are classified in the tonic area: they can, therefore, be used in a chord progression instead of the major triad on I. This, however, is almost never the case with the final chord or cadence of a piece of music. What all three chords have in common is the fact that none of them contains the fourth of the scale.

In the subdominant area we see the subdominant itself (IV) and its related minor on the second degree (II). Both triads contain the fourth of the scale. The diminished triad on the seventh degree (VII) is assigned to the dominant (V). This triad on VII may also be regarded as a "shortened" dominant seventh chord *(see Page 65, Example 21)*.

Most cadences, not only in classical music but in rock, pop and jazz as well, follow the course of a **tension curve** which moves from a stable chord (tonic area) to a less stable chord (subdominant area) and then to the height of its tension with an unstable chord (dominant area) to be then resolved again in a stable chord (tonic area) *(Example 20)*.

20

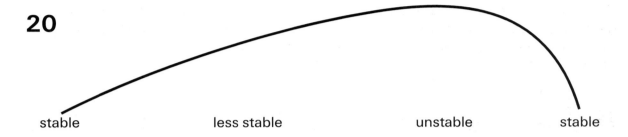

stable   less stable   unstable   stable

The following table provides an overview of how the diatonic triads are subdivided into the functional areas *(Example 21)*. This classification is not even affected by adding a further third to the diatonic triads to make them four-notes *chords (see Page 62, Example 14)*.

21

Tonic area	I IIIm VIm	stable
Subdominant area	IV IIm	less stable
Dominant area	V VII°	unstable

The Relationship Between Triads a Third Apart

The **relationship between triads a third apart** may be defined in various ways. The first definition says that all triads are related to each other in thirds as long as the roots of these triads are one third apart from each other. This leads to triads being classified as related to each other even though our ears may tell us something different. The following illustrations should help to provide an insight into the relationships a major third apart and a minor third apart *(Example 22)*.

22   Relationships a Major Third Apart   Relationships a Minor Third Apart

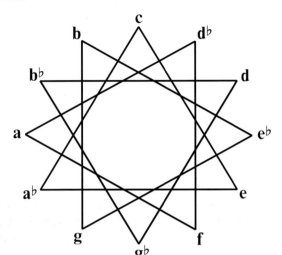
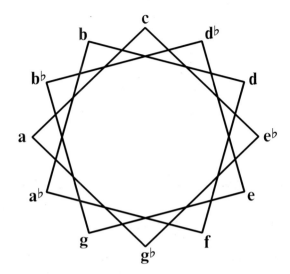

Superimposing major thirds produces four possible sequences: **c - e - g#**, **db - f - a**, **d - f# - a#** and **eb - g - b**. In classical harmony this is referred to as **mediant**, but only the major third relationship is meant. This word must have come into being by virtue of the fact that the chord on the major third **(III)** of a tonic is precisely in the middle between tonic and dominant (Late Latin mediãre = to be in the middle). In contrast, the minor thirds form only the following three sequences: **c - eb - gb - a**,   **c# - e - g - bb** and **d - f - ab - b**

The second way of defining the relationship between triads a third apart is based on two corresponding notes of the related triads. Although this severely restricts the number of possible combinations it helps us to understand the relationship of the triads concerned much better than the first way does *(Example 23)*.

23

If we want to differentiate even more precisely we can also speak of **interweaved** or **interlocking thirds**, as these triads when put on top of each other produce an interlaced, virtually uniform picture. The following triads are then related to each other in thirds (or interlocking thirds) *(Example 24)*:

24

C	to	Em	and	E°
Cm	to	E♭	and	E♭⁺
C⁺	to	E	and	E⁺
C°	to	E♭m	and	E♭°

The Diatonic Relationship

The **diatonic relationship** says that triads from the same scale are always related to each other for the simple reason that they are formed from the same tonal material *(see Example 12)*, so it is a simple matter to find suitable melodies for a random combination of such diatonic triads using the original scale. This then makes these relationships particularly important for learning the theoretical rudiments of melodic improvisation.

The Half-Tone Relationship

At this point it is necessary to draw the reader's attention to the largely unknown way of interlinking triads, which we shall call the **half-tone relationship**. The definition of this relationship says that two notes must correspond in the triads which are half-tone related to each other (as was the case with the relationship of triads a third apart) and the third note may only deviate by a half tone up or down. The following triads would then be half-tone related to, for instance, a C major triad: Em (2nd inversion), C#°, Cm and C⁺ *(Example 25)*.

25

It is best here as well to present visually in the form of a table the various possibilities of the half-tone relationship, so that specific use can be made of the ways of interlinking triads in practice *(Example 26)*.

26

triads:	are half-tone related to:						
C	Em (2nd inv.)	C#°		Cm	C+		
Cm	B+	C		C°	A♭ (1st inv.)		
C+	E (2nd inv.)	Fm (2nd inv.)	C	Am (1st inv.)		C#m	
C°	B	Cm					

Chord Symbols for Triad Inversions

If you want to write one particular inversion of a triad as a chord symbol it is best to use the standard international form. The lowest note of this inversion is added to the chord symbol as a bass note after an oblique stroke or a slash. A **Cm/G** is then a C minor chord with the note "g" in the bass, the second inversion thus being meant. The first inversion would have to be notated as **Cm/E♭** *(Example 27).*

27

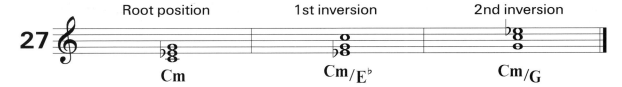

It should, however, not be automatically assumed that an unappended chord symbol invariably means a chord in the root position. There is always a certain freedom allowed the person performing the music to create his own individual interpretation by, for instance, doubling certain notes at the octave or selecting a particular inversion. It is simply not possible to lay down a set of rules as to the choice of certain **spacing** of the notes of chords. In the end, the decisive factor has got to be such things as personal taste or purely tonal aspects. If, however, the bass note does appear after the chord symbol, then you have no choice in the matter - you have to play it as it is written.

Triads with Additional Bass Note

This way of writing inversions can also be put to good use to stipulate bass notes which are actually alien to the triad. It does in effect create a chord of four notes, but it can make sense in certain situations to regard these harmonies as triads with an additional bass note. A **pedal point** is such a case. A pedal point is a bass note fixed as the lowest note for several harmonies - it just stays there, even if the chords above it change *(Example 28)*.

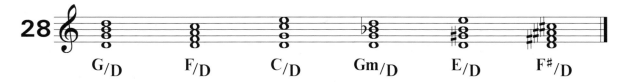

A pedal point can also be termed a **bass pedal**, a name which can be attributed to the sustaining pedal of the piano. Pedal notes are notes which are sustained for several chords. In addition to the bass pedal there is also the **melody pedal** or **inverted pedal**, where the notes sustained are melody notes, and the **inner pedal** or **middle voice pedal**, where the sustained notes are in the inner or middle voices.

Chord symbols with an additional bass note after the slash are also often termed **slash chords**, for reasons which will be abundantly apparent. As such slash chords are either an inversion of a triad (as described above) or a 4-note chord there is a detailed list of them in the chapter on chords of four notes *(see Page 61/62, Examples 12 and 13)*.

Chapter 4 Exercises

1. What are the following triads called?

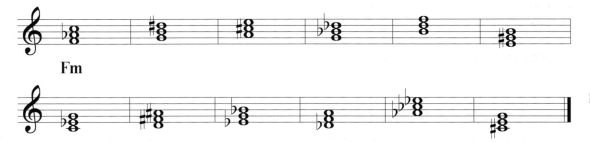

2. Write out the following triads in full.

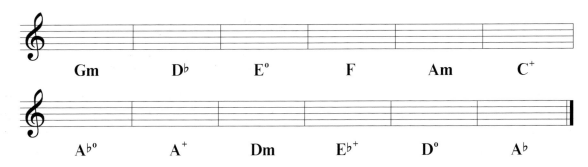

3. What are these inversions called?

C/E

4. Fill in the diatonic triads of the scale of E♭ major.

I   II   III   IV   V   VI   VII

5. Which diatonic triads are common to both the D major scale and the G major scale?

Chapter 5

Four-Note Chords and their Extensions

Chords of four notes are basically formed by extending triads by a further third, so that the four basic triads *(see Page 43/44, Examples 2 to 4)*, for instance, are each extended by a major or a minor third thus producing a series of chords with four notes. Let's now take a much closer look at these chords, arranged according to the size of their intervals *(Example 1)*.

1

The augmented triad can only be extended by a minor third as extending it by a major third would result in the root of the augmented triad again and nothing would have been changed, save for doubling the root. All the other basic triads can be extended by both the major and the minor third, producing 7 different four-note chords. We'll look at these 7 main seventh chords in the next few sections after we have dealt with chord symbols.

The Make-Up and Extension of Four-Note Chords

As we learned when dealing with the triads, all the chords are traditionally seen as thirds superimposed on top of each other. If then four-note chords are to be extended, this is also done by superimposing another third, and this can go right up to the root again 2 octaves higher *(Example 2)*.

2

15	-	is the root again	
13	-	thirteenth	(≙ 6 + octave)
11	-	eleventh	(≙ 4 + octave)
9	-	ninth	(≙ 2 + octave)
7	-	seventh	
5	-	fifth	
3	-	third	

Symbols Used to Designate Chords

Four-note chords need names which can be generally understood and it was for this reason that agreement was reached as to certain signs and additions which should be added to the triad symbols. To this end, the interval from the root to the additional notes is measured and expressed as a raised letter or number to the right of the triad symbol, which is why these additional tones are also called **index tones**. Which index symbols are assigned to which intervals can best be seen from the following **interval-index table** (Example 3).

3

Distance from Root "c"	Half-Tone Distance	Name of Interval	Sign in Chord Symbol
c - c	0	unison	root, capital letter
c - d♭	1	min. second	♭9
c - d	2	maj. second	9, add9
c - d♯	3	aug. second	♯9
c - e♭	3	min. third	m or o
c - e	4	maj. third	maj. or +
c - f	5	fourth	sus4 or 11
c - f♯	6	aug. fourth	♯11
c - g♭	6	dim. fifth	♭5, when o included
c - g	7	fifth	with pure major and minor
c - g♯	8	aug. fifth	♯5, when + included
c - a♭	8	min. sixth	♭6 or ♭13
c - a	9	major sixth	6 or 13
c - b♭♭	9	dim. seventh	o7
c - b♭	10	min. seventh	7
c - b	11	maj. seventh	maj7
c - c'	12	octave	see unison

Two Index Systems

There are two different systems for indexing these notes next to the chord symbol. The first says that any notes in the superimposed thirds which are between the fifth of the triad and the index note have to be included. This would mean, for instance, that a Dm11 chord would be a D minor triad with a minor seventh, major ninth and a perfect eleventh (Example 4).

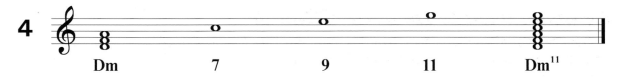

The drawback of this is that unwanted additional notes cannot be excluded in this way of writing them, which is why this system of chord symbols is being disregarded more and more. The advantage, of course, is in its succinctness, which makes it highly suitable for quickly noting something down when composing perhaps, as long as the composer does actually know which chord he really means with this abbreviated form.

The second, much more widely-spread system says that the number principally denoting the type of chord should be after the triad symbol, and in most cases it is the seventh. Any other notes needn't necessarily be given but they can be written after a slash or in brackets behind the seventh *(Example 5)*.

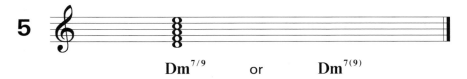

These additional notes (not the seventh) are called options. Such an **option** should most certainly be indicated if it has particular harmonic significance in the given context. Indicating all the notes wanted is, though, usually unnecessary, as it makes the chord symbols too long and as a result illegible, and the experienced musician will in any case choose the right options should the need arise. The second system is used exclusively in this book.

A widely-held misconception concerns the options in brackets. The brackets don't for instance mean that it's up to the musician which notes he plays - they all have to be played. So it is not the case that the options following a slash must be played and the ones in brackets can be played. These two ways of writing chords both enjoy equal status and in fact the trend is moving away from making any distinctions at all *(Example 6)*.

10 General Rules for Chord Symbols

You should consider the following rules when "decoding" or "encoding" such chord symbols. They are essential when you want to work with the interval-index table:

1. The index numbers are written raised and to the right of the chord symbol in order of their magnitude.

2. The seventh (if in the chord) should always be placed first.

3. If a chord has both a sixth and a seventh, the symbol for the sixth (6) is put an octave higher and becomes a thirteenth "13". The sixth of the chord can nevertheless be below the seventh. This rule was introduced to have the seventh invariably first in the chord symbol.

4. The options "♭5", "♯5" and "sus4" should always come at the end of a chord symbol. The optional notes "♭5" and "♯5" replace the perfect fifth (5) normally found in a major or minor chord. Diminished and perfect fifths are never found together in one chord.

5. The chord C^5 is commonly called a **power chord**, and it contains just the root (c) and the fifth (g), the third simply being left out. The question of whether the missing third suggests a minor or major chord is left open. The mode of this chord is deliberately not fixed.

6. Having "add9" after the chord symbol means that only the ninth should be played in this chord and never the seventh as well. The major ninth is then simply added to the triad symbol. You may even occasionally see "add11" chords too.

7. The symbol "^{07}" always refers to both the diminished triad (X^0) and the diminished seventh (^{07}). A X^{07} chord thus denotes a diminished seventh chord consisting only of minor thirds *(Example 7)*.

8. In most cases the options "♯11" and "♭13" are treated in the same way as the enharmonically synonymous symbols "♭5" and "♯5", which explains the frequent omission of the perfect fifth because of the sound created in chords with these options *(see Rule No. 4)*. This should, however, be scrutinised on a case to case basis.

9. The option "sus **4**" is used only in major chords. The fourth is so to speak suspended before the third so that the latter is omitted *(Example 8)*. Logically enough it is called a **suspended fourth**, but it does not necessarily mean that it has to be resolved onto the major third, as was the practice in baroque harmony. The sus**4** chord should instead be regarded as a tonal structure in its own right. In all other cases the perfect fourth appears as "**11**".

10. The option "7/alt." mostly stands for the typical **altered chord** sound "7/♯9/♭13" *(Example 9)*. There is closer examination of the subject of altered chords and altered scales in the chapter on the melodic minor *(see Vol.I, P 94 ff. and Vol.II, P 45ff., 84/85, 102 ff.)*.

The 7 Main Seventh Chords

If we look at the interval table and its rules we can see that the four-note chords in Example 1 of this chapter are called $C^{maj7/\sharp 5}$, C^{maj7}, C^7, Cm^{maj7}, Cm^7, $Cm^{7/\flat 5}$ and C^{o7} *(Example 10)*. These 7 four-note chords may also be regarded as the **main** or **primary seventh chords** as they are formed by superimposing thirds and the origins of all other 4-note chords as well as of all 4-note chord extensions can be traced back to these 7 main types. We will later see that all diatonic seventh chords of the most important scales belong to the primary chords shown here.

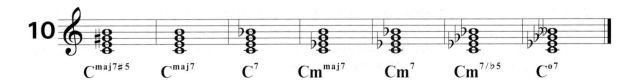

How to Decipher Chord Symbols

Unknown chord symbols can be unravelled to reveal their individual notes, thus enabling them to be actually played. The first thing to do is to find out which triad is the basis of the chord. With straight major and minor chords this doesn't present a problem: capital letters represent major triads and a small "**m**" tagged on to these capital letters means it is a minor chord *(see P 45, Examples 10 and 11)*. The next thing we should look at is the seventh (if it is there). A major seventh is shown as "maj7" and a minor simply as "7". This is, by the way, the only case where a minor interval is written without a flat accidental before the index number (so it's never ♭7, just 7).

The last thing we have to do is calculate the remaining add-ons or options to the chord symbol starting from the root using the interval-index table *(Example 3)*. At this point, however, you should perhaps refresh your memory of the 10 rules for the chord symbols as there are some special features in the way of writing them that may lead to some of the notes which you have so laboriously deciphered from the chord having to be deleted. Rereading the relevant rules is a prerequisite for the following types of chords: ♭5, ♯5, ♯11, ♭13, o7 and sus4. There are some exercises on this at the end of the chapter.

How to Put Notes Together to Form a Chord Symbol

The reverse of the procedure described above proves to be far more difficult, as there are several ways of describing a group of notes in the form of a chord symbol. The trick here is to track down the root of the chord because all the other notes can then be determined using the interval-index table. The easiest way of finding the root is to try to get the notes back to their original layers of thirds by **transposing** them by an octave up or down *(Example 2)*. The root is then usually the lowest of these.

Four-Note Chords as Triads with an Additional Bass Note

We have already seen when dealing with triads that for certain reasons 4-note chords can also be notated as triads with an additional bass note. You might, for instance, be notating for a pianist who can play the bass note with his left hand and put the triad on top of it with his right. Or you might want to divide up the notes of the chord among several instruments e.g. bass and guitar, and in such cases this way of writing them is far easier to read, especially as pedal points or fundamentals can be spotted more easily *(see P 53, Example 28)*. The triads used in such cases are as a rule straight major and minor triads, which of course also simplifies reading them considerably *(Example 11)*.

11

Em/C	E♭/C	D/C	D♭/C	C

Slash Chords

I have mentioned already that triads with an additional bass note are also termed "slash chords" *(see P 53)*. In principle, any chord can have an additional bass note tagged on to it but in practice it is mostly only major and minor triads. Such slash chords can be simple inversions of these major and minor triads whereas in other cases they may be just 4-note chords which for certain reasons are written as a triad with an additional bass note *(see above)*. On occasions, though, completely new sounds are created as well. The following list provides an overview of all the slash chords with major and minor triads *(Examples 12 and 13)*.

12

C/C	C major triad	(triad)
D♭/C	$D^{♭maj7}$ seventh chord with the seventh in the bass	(inversion)
D/C	D^7 seventh chord with the seventh in the bass	(inversion)
E♭/C	Cm^7 seventh chord	(seventh chord)
E/C	$C^{maj7/♯5}$ seventh chord	(seventh chord)
F/C	F major triad with the fifth in the bass	(inversion)
F♯/C	$C^{7/♭9/♯11}$ without the third	(new)
G/C	$C^{maj7/9}$ or $Cm^{maj7/9}$ without the third	(new)
A♭/C	A♭ major triad with the third in the bass	(inversion)
A/C	$C^{7/♭9/13}$ without the fifth and the seventh	(new)
B♭/C	$C^{7/9/sus4}$ without the fifth and the seventh	(new)
B/C	$B^{7/♭9}$ without the seventh, ♭9 in the bass	(new)

13

Cm/C	C minor triad	(triad)
$D\flat m/C$	$D\flat m^{maj7}$ seventh chord with the seventh in the bass	(inversion)
Dm/C	Dm^{7} seventh chord with the seventh in the bass	(inversion)
$E\flat m/C$	$Cm^{7/\flat5}$ seventh chord	(seventh chord)
Em/C	C^{maj7} seventh chord	(seventh chord)
Fm/C	F minor triad with the fifth in the bass	(inversion)
$F\sharp m/C$	no alternative description	(new)
Gm/C	$C^{7/9}$ or $Cm^{7/9}$ without the third or $C^{7/9/sus4}$ without ^{sus4}	(new)
$G\sharp m/C$	no alternative description	(new)
Am/C	A minor triad with the third in the bass	(inversion)
$B\flat m/C$	$C^{7/\flat9/sus4}$ without the fifth	(new)
Bm/C	$D^{7/13}$ without the fifth with the seventh in the bass	(new)

The Diatonic Seventh Chords of a Major Scale

If you superimpose another third on the triads which are on the separate degrees of a major scale *(see Page 46, Example 13)* you automatically get the **diatonic seventh chords** of a major scale *(Example 14)*, the one precondition being that the fourth note is likewise taken from that major scale.

14

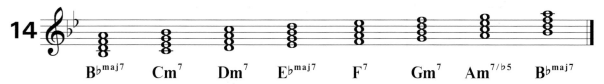

$$B\flat^{maj7} \quad Cm^{7} \quad Dm^{7} \quad E\flat^{maj7} \quad F^{7} \quad Gm^{7} \quad Am^{7/\flat5} \quad B\flat^{maj7}$$

These diatonic seventh chords can be formed in any major key with the following general formula by replacing the Roman numerals of the degree symbols by the notes of the major scale required *(Example 15)*:

15

$$I^{maj7} \quad IIm^{7} \quad IIIm^{7} \quad IV^{maj7} \quad V^{7} \quad VIm^{7} \quad VIIm^{7/\flat5}$$

The Cadence of the Diatonic Seventh Chords in Fourths

Just as is the case with the diatonic triads, these diatonic 4-note chords are also related to each other by virtue of the fact that they come from the same scale. It is therefore possible to combine these seventh chords with each other in a harmonic context and to obtain tonally satisfactory results (just try it out for yourself). If you proceed from the first degree to each diatonic chord a fifth below or a fourth above you get a cadence of all the 7 harmonies concerned *(Example 16)*:

16 | I^{maj7} | IV^{maj7} | $VIIm^{7/b5}$ | $IIIm^7$ | VIm^7 | IIm^7 | V^7 | I^{maj7} |

We might call this cadence the **cadence in fourths** of the **diatonic seventh chords**, because of the intervals of fourths of the roots, but it is simpler just to say a **diatonic cadence**. One of the reasons it sounds so scorrevole or flowing and conclusive is that each chord has two notes in common with both the chord before it and the one after it: it so to speak forms an unending chord chain *(Example 17)*:

17
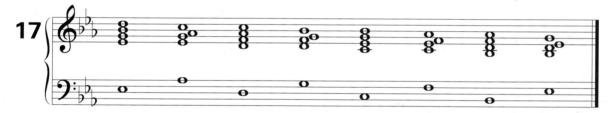

In-depth study of harmonic relationships will frequently reveal this cadence, albeit generally in an abbreviated form. The most common of these shorter cadences are *(Example 18)*:

18

II	V			
V	I			
II	V	I		
II	V	I	IV	
VI	II	V	I	
III	VI	II	V	I

These progressions crop up so often that it is fair to speak of **chord clichés**. These cadence formulae are dealt with in detail in Volume II of The New Theory of Harmony in the chapters on the **II**-**V**-**I** progression *(Vol. II, pp. 10 ff., 29 ff. and 63 ff.)*.

Chord Synonyms

These are 4-note chords or extended 4-note chords that have a different root and whose chord symbol is therefore different but they nevertheless are made up of the same notes. A simple illustration of this are the 4-note chords of C^6 and Am^7. Both are made up of the notes c, e, g and a, the only difference being the choice of the root. The root is, however, of paramount importance as regards the treatment of chords in functional relationships, which is why we should be most wary of randomly interchanging the chord synonyms listed below *(Example 19)*.

19

C^6	has the same notes as	Am^7
Cm^7	"	$E\flat^6$
Cm^6	"	$Am^{7/\flat5}$
$Cm^{7/\flat5}$	"	$E\flat m^6$
$C^{7/\flat5}$	"	$G\flat^{7/\flat5}$
C^{o7}	"	$E\flat^{o7}, G\flat^{o7}$ und A^{o7}
C^+	"	E^+ und $G^{\sharp+}$
$C^{6/9}$	"	$Am^{7/11}$
$Cm^{7/11}$	"	$E\flat^{6/9}$
$Cm^{6/9}$	"	$Am^{7/11/\flat5}$
$Cm^{7/11/\flat5}$	"	$E\flat m^{6/9}$

Shortened Four-Note Chords

These are 4-note chords whose root has been "cut", thus becoming triads. Such situations arise in the main when splitting up individual chord parts among various instruments or when separating the root from the rest of the chord. This term is also used to describe the relationship between 3-note and 4-note chords, so an A minor triad, for instance, can also be seen as a cut F^{maj7} or as a cut $F^{\sharp}m^{7/\flat5}$ seventh chord *(Example 20)*.

20

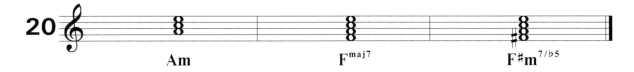

Am F^{maj7} $F^{\sharp}m^{7/\flat5}$

We can see then that the triad of $\mathbf{Am}$ is in both the $\mathbf{F}^{maj7}$ and the $\mathbf{F^{\#}m}^{7/b5}$ chord. If the 7 main seventh chords are cut, i.e. the root is taken away, the result is always triads *(Example 21)*.

21

$\mathbf{C}^{maj7/\#5}$	contains	$\mathbf{E}$
$\mathbf{C}^{maj7}$	"	$\mathbf{Em}$
$\mathbf{C}^{7}$	"	$\mathbf{E^{o}}$
$\mathbf{Cm}^{maj7}$	"	$\mathbf{E^{b+}}$
$\mathbf{Cm}^{7}$	"	$\mathbf{E^{b}}$
$\mathbf{Cm}^{7/b5}$	"	$\mathbf{E^{b}m}$
$\mathbf{C}^{o7}$	"	$\mathbf{E^{bo}}$

The Relationships of Four-Note Chords a Third Apart

The definition of the relationship of 4-note chords a third apart is that three of the four notes of these chords should correspond and their root must be a third apart. This results in a wealth of related 4-note chords a third apart.

We can, however, take this definition even further and say that the note that is not the same must also produce a musically meaningful additional tone seen from the root of the related chord or must represent one of the usual options of this chord. The interesting thing here is primarily the fact that two 4-note chords whose roots are a third apart can together result in a 5-note chord. These 4-note chords may be regarded as 4-note chords interlocked in thirds *(Example 22)*.

22
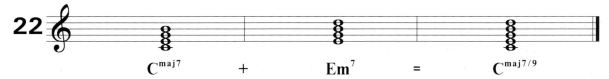

$\mathbf{C}^{maj7}$ + $\mathbf{Em}^{7}$ = $\mathbf{C}^{maj7/9}$

All these definitions lead to the great number of theoretically possible related chords a third apart being limited and hence they become clearer. If the relationship of 4-note chords a third apart is so narrowly defined as described above it is limited to the following 4-note chords "interlocked in thirds", whose notes taken together then form a five-note chord *(Example 23)*.

23

C^{maj7}	and	Em^7	produce	$C^{maj7/9}$
$C^{7/\sharp 5}$	"	$E^{maj7/\sharp 5}$	"	$C^{7/\sharp 9/\flat 13}$
C^7	"	$Em^{7/\flat 5}$	"	$C^{7/9}$
C^7	"	E^{o7}	"	$C^{7/\flat 9}$
Cm^{maj7}	"	$E\flat^{maj7/\sharp 5}$	"	$Cm^{maj7/9}$
Cm^7	"	$E\flat^{maj7}$	"	$Cm^{7/9}$
$Cm^{7/\flat 5}$	"	$E\flat m^{maj7}$	"	$Cm^{7/9/\flat 5}$
C^{o7}	"	$E\flat^{o7}$	"	C^{o7}

If we leave out this restriction we get the following result: each 4-note chord is related in thirds to the triad that is in it *(Example 21)*, as well as to the 4-note chords that result from extending this triad. For instance, a C^{maj7} chord would be related to the E minor triad within it and to the 4-note chords of Em^6, Em^7 and Em^{maj7} *(Example 24)*.

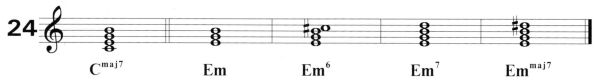

24 C^{maj7} Em Em^6 Em^7 Em^{maj7}

When comparing the sound of the chords the closer relationship of the Em^7 chord to the C^{maj7} immediately becomes apparent. This can be put down to the fact already mentioned above that the seventh "d" of the Em^7 seventh chord is a major ninth (**9**) seen from the C^{maj7} point of view, and can certainly serve as a further option for a C^{maj7} chord. The sixth "c$^\sharp$" and the major seventh "d$^\sharp$" on the other hand do not go with C^{maj7} as a minor ninth ($\flat$9) or an augmented ninth ($\sharp$9).

Half-Tone Related Four-Note Chords

These should be treated in the same way as the half-tone-related triads *(see Pp 51/52, Examples 25 and 26)*. Half tone differences between the options are not meant here but just the half-tone relationship between the notes of the basic 4-note chord; a $D^{7/9}$ chord, for instance, is half-tone related to the chords $Dm^{7/9}$ and $D^{maj7/9}$. The half tone difference is from the major third to the minor third (from $D^{7/9}$ to $Dm^{7/9}$) or from the minor seventh to the major seventh (from $D^{7/9}$ to $D^{maj7/9}$). However, the chord $D^{7/\flat 9}$ is not half-tone related to the $D^{7/9}$ chord. The half-tone difference from the major to the minor ninth is with the optional note in this case *(Example 25)*.

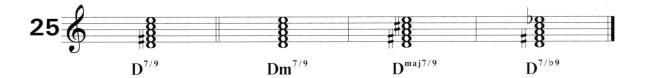

25

$D^{7/9}$ $Dm^{7/9}$ $D^{maj7/9}$ $D^{7/\flat 9}$

The definition of half-tone relationships between 4-note chords is then, that each of the notes of the basic 4-note chord may change a half tone up or down, and this applies to the root as well. If we take a look at the half-tone relationships between the seven main 4-note chords we see a whole gamut of ways for combining these chords with each other, some of which are quite remarkable.

26

4-note chord	half-tone related to
$C^{maj7/\sharp 5}$	$C\sharp m^7$, $C^{7/\sharp 5}$, C^{maj7}, C^+
C^{maj7}	$C\sharp m^{7/\flat 5}$, $C^{maj7/\sharp 5}$, C^7, Cm^{maj7}
Cm^{maj7}	C^{maj7}, Cm^7, B^+
C^7	$C\sharp^{o7}$, C^{maj7}, $C^{7/\sharp 5}$, $C^{7/\flat 5}$, $C^{7/sus4}$, C^6, Cm^7
Cm^7	C^7, Cm^{maj7}, $Cm^{7/\flat 5}$, Cm^6, $B^{maj7/\sharp 5}$
$Cm^{7/\flat 5}$	$C^{7/\flat 5}$, Cm^7, C^{o7}, B^{maj7}
C^{o7}	$Cm^{7/\flat 5}$, Cm^6, B^7

Chapter 5 Exercises

1. What are the following 4-note chords called?

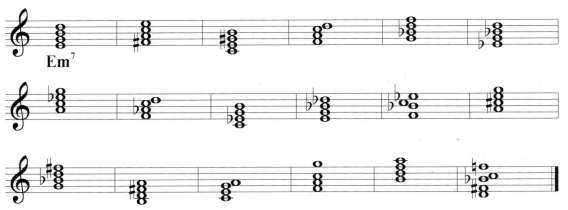

Em^7

2. Fill in the notes for each of the following chord symbols.

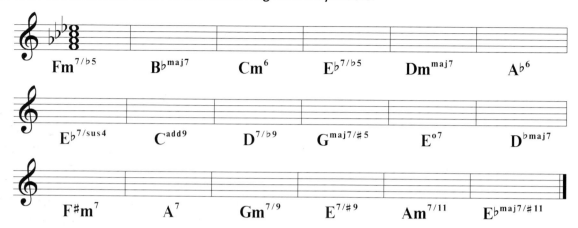

$Fm^{7/\flat5}$ $B\flat^{maj7}$ Cm^6 $E\flat^{7/\flat5}$ Dm^{maj7} $A\flat^6$

$E\flat^{7/sus4}$ C^{add9} $D^{7/\flat9}$ $G^{maj7/\sharp5}$ E^{o7} $D\flat^{maj7}$

$F\sharp m^7$ A^7 $Gm^{7/9}$ $E^{7/\sharp9}$ $Am^{7/11}$ $E\flat^{maj7/\sharp11}$

3. Write the diatonic seventh chords of the scale of $A\flat$ major.

$A\flat^{maj7}$

4. Find the roots of these chords and add the correct chord symbol.

a.   b.   c.   d.

C^6, Am^7

5. The triads with an additional bass note (P 53, Example 28) can partly be notated as 4-note chords.

Chapter 6
The Ionian System

Not only can a chord be assigned to each separate degree of a major scale, but each degree can have its own scale as well. These scales are made up of the 7 notes of the major scale but they begin with the fundamental tone of the degree *(Example 1)*. These **scales of the degrees** owe their names to the Greek scales in the diatonic "systema teleion" from the eighth century, which were named after Greek tribes. In the Middle Ages they were classified into six (later twelve) "octave species" on the Greek pattern and as so-called **church** or **ecclesiastical modes** they were endowed with the names of the Greek scales. In the Middle Ages these church modes were more or less the equivalent of our present day major and minor.

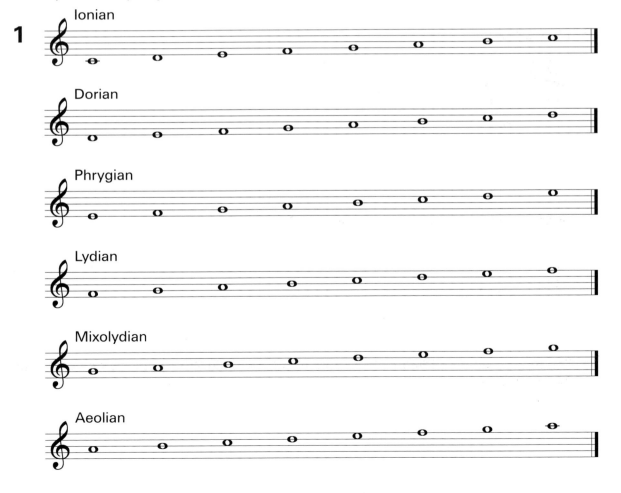

From the Church Modes to the Ionian System

With the introduction of the well-tempered tuning and the major-minor system, which offers much greater scope for modulation *(see P 29)*, the church modes were replaced by the major- minor system in the 17th century. Yet it was above all the field of jazz harmony that saw the church modes achieving a new significant role in the 20th century. The old **modes** became the vehicles for completely new styles of creative improvisation (chiefly in "modal" jazz). These six church modes, which are on the first six degrees of a major scale, were supplemented by the Locrian scale on the VIIth degree, thereby making the system complete. The major scale in this system is called the "**Ionian scale**", which is why this whole chord-scale system is named after it. The present day Ionian system may thus be regarded as an integral part of the major-minor system, which in its turn gains in the richness of variety it offers.

Chords are Scales - Scales are Chords

The Ionian system can serve as a basis to explain the **chord-scale theory**. This theory says that in principle no distinction needs to be made between chords and the scales belonging to them because both are made up of the same notes. Chords and scales are thus treated equally. Chords are seen as **vertical tonal structures** (mostly in superimposed thirds) which may be represented in the form of scales (at intervals of a second) arranged horizontally *(Example 2)*. The way of purely seeing chords in conventional harmony as rigid vertical structures must be regarded as obsolete from a contemporary point of view.

$C^{maj7/9/\sharp 11/13}$

A Closed Tonal System

The complete Ionian system starts from a major scale and contains first of all 7 separate scales which are built on the 7 degrees of a major scale using the notes of this major scale. It also contains the seventh chords belonging to the individual scales, these chords being identical to the diatonic seventh chords of the major scale concerned. 3 options (additional notes), which likewise come from the scale concerned, are assigned to these seventh chords. The four notes of the seventh chord together with the three optional notes form the 7 notes of that scale *(Example 3)*.

3

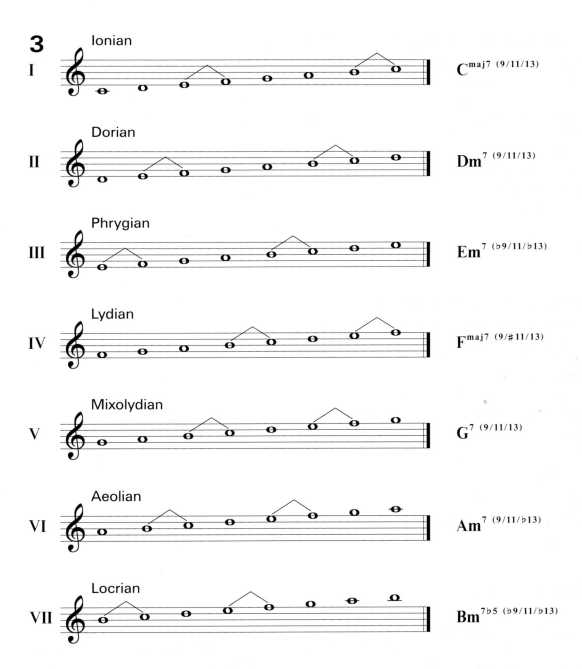

I	Ionian	C$^{maj7\ (9/11/13)}$
II	Dorian	Dm$^{7\ (9/11/13)}$
III	Phrygian	Em$^{7\ (\flat9/11/\flat13)}$
IV	Lydian	F$^{maj7\ (9/\sharp11/13)}$
V	Mixolydian	G$^{7\ (9/11/13)}$
VI	Aeolian	Am$^{7\ (9/11/\flat13)}$
VII	Locrian	Bm$^{7\flat5\ (\flat9/11/\flat13)}$

We see then that the 7 notes of a scale can be divided into two groups: on the one hand we have the four notes forming the seventh chord of the scale and on the other we see the three optional notes *(Example 4)*.

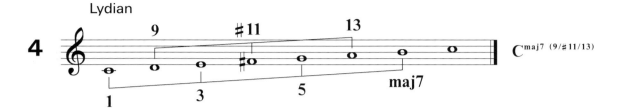

Scale Structures

The scales of the Ionian system can - in keeping with the significance of the church modes in the Middle Ages - be regarded as scales and tonal structures in their own right and with their own character. It is necessary here to free these scales from their origin in the major scale and to use them in any way you like in all the keys. This aim can best be achieved in practice by introducing absolute scale structures. The simplest way of doing this is to remember the position of the half-tone steps because then you can form the scale you want from any keynote you care to start with *(Example 5)*.

5

Ionian	3 ⌢ 4	7 ⌢ 8
Dorian	2 ⌢ 3	6 ⌢ 7
Phrygian	1 ⌢ 2	5 ⌢ 6
Lydian	4 ⌢ 5	7 ⌢ 8
Mixolydian	3 ⌢ 4	6 ⌢ 7
Aeolian	2 ⌢ 3	5 ⌢ 6
Locrian	1 ⌢ 2	4 ⌢ 5

Scale structures can also be made clear by using the major scale as a model. The notes of a major scale are given the numbers from 1 to 8. If certain notes differ in another scale these divergences are marked with accidentals. The simplest way of comparing the seven scales of the Ionian system with each other is to write them out one after the other using the same keynote *(Example 6)*.

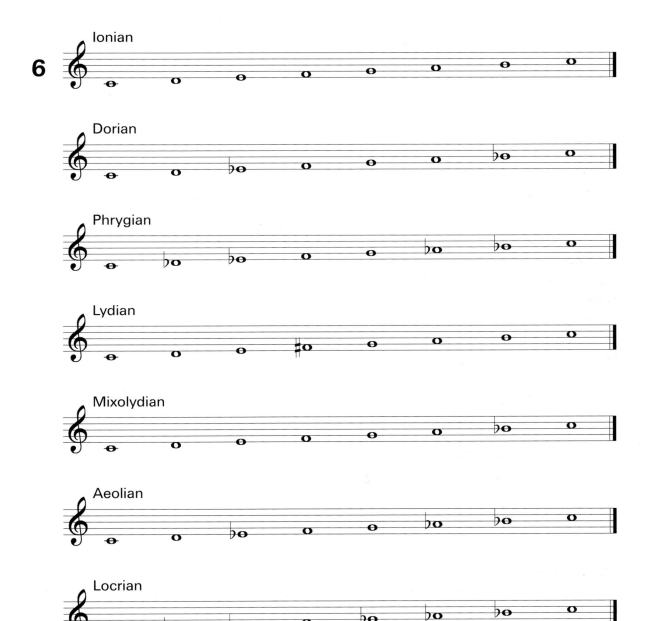

The scales of the Ionian system thus feature the following structures.

7

	1	2	3	4	5	6	7	8
Ionian	1	2	3	4	5	6	7	8
Dorian	1	2	♭3	4	5	6	♭7	8
Phrygian	1	♭2	♭3	4	5	♭6	♭7	8
Lydian	1	2	3	♯4	5	6	7	8
Mixolydian	1	2	3	4	5	6	♭7	8
Aeolian	1	2	♭3	4	5	♭6	♭7	8
Locrian	1	♭2	♭3	4	♭5	♭6	♭7	8

This system is beautifully straight forward in that direct comparisons can be made between the individual scales and they are readily comprehensible. The one disadvantage of this system is that in the case of the seventh, the absolute symbol for the note of the scale does not correspond to the way of writing the chord symbols, as a minor seventh is notated as " 7 " and not as " ♭7 ", and a major seventh as " **maj7** " and not as " 7 ". The usual way of writing the chord symbols can, however, also be used with scales to fix the absolute pitch *(Example 8)*.

8

	1	9	3	11	5	13	maj7	1
Ionian	1	9	3	11	5	13	maj7	1
Dorian	1	9	♭3	11	5	13	7	1
Phrygian	1	♭9	♭3	11	5	♭13	7	1
Lydian	1	9	3	♯11	5	13	maj7	1
Mixolydian	1	9	3	11	5	13	7	1
Aeolian	1	9	♭3	11	5	♭13	7	1
Locrian	1	♭9	♭3	11	♭5	♭13	7	1

Scale Relationships

Although it is quite apparent that the scales of the Ionian system derived from a common scale are closely related to each other, I would like at this point to draw your attention to the half-tone relationship that is also found with scales. Scales are half-tone related to each other if just one of their (generally) seven notes is different by a half tone and the remaining 6 notes are identical. These half-tone-related scales may be put together into pairs of scales with the same fundamental tone, and in practice they are, under certain circumstances, interchangeable. It goes really without saying that when there is a subtle change in the make-up of the scale, certain passages in a composition merge with each other better than if there were, for instance, an abrupt change of the notes selected. The following table shows each of the half-tone-related pairs of scales of the Ionian system *(Example 9)*.

9

Ionian	- Lydian	($11/\sharp 11$)
Ionian	- Mixolydian	($\text{maj}7/7$)
Dorian	- Aeolian	($13/\flat 13$)
Dorian	- Mixolydian	($\flat 3/3$)
Aeolian	- Phrygian	($9/\flat 9$)
Phrygian	- Locrian	($5/\flat 5$)

(The different notes are written in brackets in chord symbol script)

The New Order

If we take this a step further and re-order the seven scales of the Ionian system according to their half-tone relationships we get the so-called "new order" of the scales of the Ionian system, as shown on the following page. We start with the Lydian scale because this (seen from the keynote of the scale) has the largest intervals. We gradually work down half tone by half tone to the Locrian scale, which, as we know, has the smallest intervals. If we now lower the keynote of the Locrian scale by half a tone we get a Lydian scale again whose fundamental tone is half a tone lower *(see Vol. II, the Diatonic Modulation Table)*.

10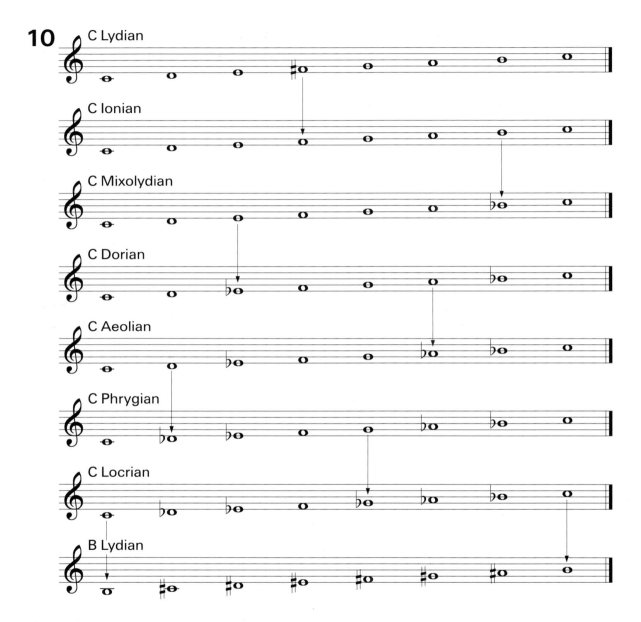

The "Avoid Notes"

The scales of the Ionian system match their corresponding seventh chords exactly, which - with three options added - are made up of the very same notes. In musical practice, however, it turns out that certain options can embellish the original seventh chord admirably, whilst other options sound nothing short of horrendous. This usually turns out to be the case when these options form a dissonant interval with a note already in the seventh chord, thereby rendering them unable in practice to be used as a note of the chord. For instance, a C^{maj7} 4-note chord can be embellished by the options "9" and "13" contained in its Ionian scale, but the "11" in this major scale makes the somewhat charming character of this chord sound dissonant *(Example* 11). This can be attributed to the very much dissonant interval of the minor ninth ($\flat$9) that is between the third of the chord and the option "11".

These notes contained in a scale, which admittedly cannot really be used as notes of a chord, are called "avoid notes". We should regard them as notes which in certain musical contexts may be used sparingly, for instance as notes of a chord or as stressed melody notes of long duration *(Example* 12).

12

Scale	avoid notes
Ionian	11
Dorian	13
Phrygian	$\flat$9, $\flat$13
Mixolydian	11 (with dominant seventh chords)
Mixolydian	3 (with sus4 chords)
Aeolian	$\flat$13
Locrian	$\flat$9

What we actually do with these avoid notes must also be seen in a wider context, for it is indeed possible that notes I have listed here as to be avoided, can nevertheless in certain contexts be used as melody notes. And at the same time even more reasons can be found to the ones above to avoid these notes within extended chord progressions.

Chapter 6 Exercises

1. Name the following scales.

a.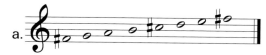

b.

c.

d.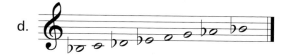

2. Write out the following scales.

a.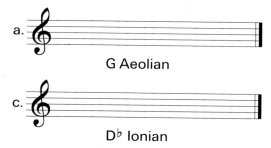

       G Aeolian

b.

       A Lydian

c.

       D♭ Ionian

d.

       F Dorian

3. Write out the Ionian system in the key of E♭ major.

4. Relationships of scales

a. Which scales are half-tone related to D Dorian?
b. And which to G Lydian?

Chapter 7
The Circle of Fifths

Since the introduction of the major-minor system the circle of fifths has been one of the most frequently used aids to harmony. It can reveal a great deal of information about different keys, accidentals and diatonic chords as well as chord and scale relationships.

The Relationship of the Tetrachords

The formation of the circle of fifths may be explained as follows: if we take a closer look at the scale of C major we notice that it can be divided into two halves of 4 notes each. These series of four notes have been called **tetrachords** since the times of the ancient Greeks ("tetra" is Greek for "four"). The two tetrachords of the C major scale have the same structure - two whole tones followed by a half tone *(Example 1)*.

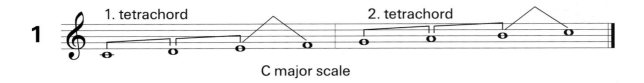

C major scale

The upper tetrachord starts on the fifth of the scale. As these two series of four notes display the same structure it seems reasonable to form a new scale from the tonic of the upper tetrachord, this fundamental note being a fifth from the keynote of the first scale. The sequence of notes is then simply continued upwards *(Example 2)*.

From C Major to G Major

In order that the half-tone structure of a major scale may at the same time be maintained with this scale starting on the note "g", the seventh note must be raised by a half tone, as otherwise the second half tone of this scale would be between the 6th and 7th degree (as in Example 2), and not between the 7th and 8th degree, where the second half tone of a major scale has to be *(see P 15, Example 9)*. In our example then, the note "**f**" has to be raised to an "**f**♯" to be able to transform the scale with the keynote "**g**" into a major scale *(Example 3)*. By using a sharp before the note "**f**" we thus produce a G major scale from the tonal elements of a C major scale. These two scales are related to each other in fifths as their keynotes are a fifth apart.

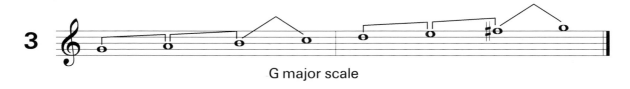

G major scale

The Circle Closes

The G major scale can now be put through the very same procedure. By continuing the upper tetrachord of the G major scale and adding another sharp we arrive at the scale of D major *(Example 4)*.

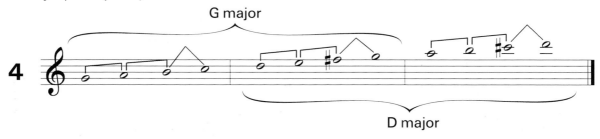

Because the seventh note of the scale is raised each time, the number of accidentals thus increases by one sharp with each additional key. This would, though - with 12 possible keynotes of major scales (an octave has 12 half tones) - be a magnificent 12 sharps by the time we had arrived at the key of B♯ major (≙ C major), even though there are but 7 notes in a scale. The circle of keys may have been closed but the practice of ever raising the notes and creating ever more sharps and double sharps would seem to be a little impractical if not downright awkward.

This can be got round by regarding the lower tetrachord of the C major scale as the upper tetrachord of a scale ending on the note "**f**". In order that an F major scale may be formed, the lower tetrachord of this F major scale now has to be changed slightly and we soon see that the fourth note of the lower tetrachord has to be lowered by half a tone so that the half-tone structure of a major scale is maintained. This then necessitates making the "**b**" into a "**b♭**" *(Example 5)*.

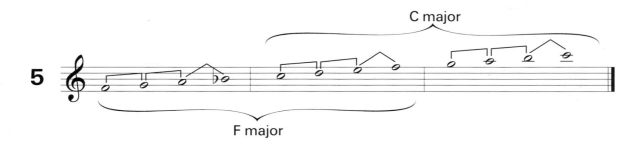

This process too can be continued in exactly the same way as the one described before so that a flat accidental is added to each new key because the fourth of the scale has to be lowered each time *(Example 6)*.

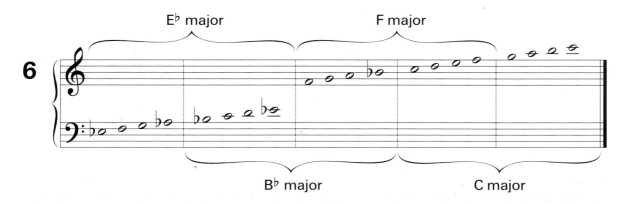

We don't want to end up with 12 flat accidentals when we get to D♭♭ major (≙ C maj.) so we agree to meet in the middle at G♭ and F♯ majors, thereby dividing the resultant circle of keys in a ♯ and a ♭ half *(see next page, Example 7)* and leading to the terms **sharp keys** and **flat keys**.

7

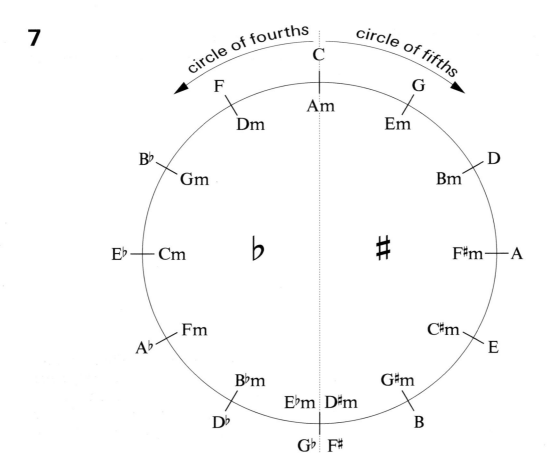

The Circle of Fifths as the Touchstone of Relationships

Immediately adjacent keys in the circle of fifths may be regarded as being closely related to each other. The further apart the keys are in the circle of fifths, the less related they become to each other. The greatest degree of relationship is the **major-minor relationship**. The sixth degree of a major scale is the fundamental tone of its related minor key, which means therefore that the Aeolian scale *(see P 69)* becomes the scale of the related minor key. In classical harmony it is known as the **natural minor**. Related keys get by on the same notes in their scales *(Example 8)* and as a result are written together in the circle of fifths, with the circle of the major keys on the outside and that of the minor keys on the inside.

8

The Diatonic Chords in the Circle of Fifths

The diatonic chords of all the keys are in close proximity to each other in the circle of fifths. For instance the first six diatonic triads of D major (**D, Em, F♯m, G, A** and **Bm**) are grouped around the tonic D major in the circle of fifths *(Example 9)*.

9

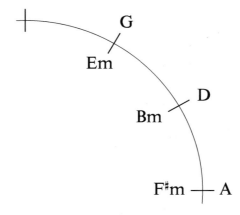

It is only the diminished triad on **VII** that evades us here as the circle of fifths does not allow inclusion of diminished triads. Using the circle of fifths we can then quickly determine whether a triad is related to another one or if these triads are indeed diatonic chords of the same major or minor scale. And the diatonic seventh chords of all the major keys can just as easily be found again in the circle of fifths using a general formula *(Example 10)*.

10

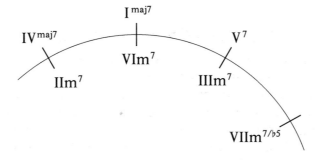

We just put the seventh chord symbol I^{maj7} of the example above in the circle of fifths on the fundamental tone of the key whose seventh chords we are trying to find out and then simply read off the resultant seventh chord symbols. Even the diatonic chord on the seventh degree can be ascertained, as being a seventh chord it is notated with the symbol "$m^{7/b5}$" and all the minor chords, unlike the diminished chords, are contained in the circle of fifths.

The Keys and Their Accidentals

It is a simple matter to read off the number of accidentals for each key with the circle of fifths. C major and A minor are "neutral" and therefore have no accidentals. Proceeding clockwise we always get one sharp more, and going anti-clockwise the number of flats increases. When we arrive at G♭ major and E♭ minor or F♯ major and D♯ minor we have reached, with 6 flats or 6 sharps, the maximum number of accidentals. It is after the clef and before the time signature that these accidentals are placed. The order of sharps in the circle of fifths going clockwise is: **f♯, c♯, g♯, d♯, a♯** and **e♯** *(Example 11)*.

We can see that every new sharp is always a half tone below the keynote of the major key concerned. The order of flats in the circle of fifths going anti-clockwise is: **b♭, e♭, a♭, d♭, g♭** and **c♭** *(Example 12)*. We see here that every new flat corresponds to the keynote of the following major key in the circle of fifths (going anti-clockwise).

The Circle of Fourths

As most of the common chord progressions and chord clichés are in fourths *(see P 63, Examples 16 to 18)* notating the circle of fifths as a circle of fourths has found favour so that these facts can be better illustrated. The sharp keys basically change places with the flat keys and the keys move upwards going clockwise by a fourth *(Example 13)*.

13

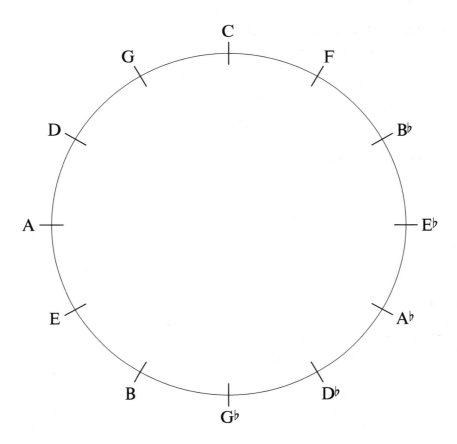

The Circle-of-Fourths Exercise

I would like at this point to present the **circle-of-fourths exercise** so that it is easier to remember as many as possible of the most important chord progressions in all keys. This exercise contains the sequence in fourths of the diatonic chords of a major scale with the degrees **II - V - I - IV** *(compare P 63, Examples 16 to 18)* in all the major and minor keys. The thing that becomes apparent is that all the harmonies in this exercise are a perfect or augmented fourth apart.

The first key with the diatonic chords of $\mathbf{Dm}^7$ $\mathbf{G}^7$ $\mathbf{C}^{maj7}$ $\mathbf{F}^{maj7}$ is C major. There then follows the relative minor key of A minor with the diatonic chords of $\mathbf{Bm}^{7/b5}$ $\mathbf{E}^7$ $\mathbf{Am}^7$ $\mathbf{D}^7$ and after that the next key in the circle of fourths is F major with the diatonic chords of $\mathbf{Gm}^7$ $\mathbf{C}^7$ $\mathbf{F}^{maj7}$ $\mathbf{Bb}^{maj7}$. It is introduced by the above chords of $\mathbf{Am}^7$ and $\mathbf{D}^7$, which have the same relationship to $\mathbf{Gm}^7$ as $\mathbf{IIm}^7$ $\mathbf{V}^7$ do to $\mathbf{Im}^7$. Here as well, each chord is a fourth apart. This all produces the effect of an infinite series of chains of these harmonies through all the keys *(Example 14)*. For further information on this subject I would refer the reader to the second volume of this work *(Vol.II, P 63 ff.)*.

14

$\mathbf{Dm}^7$	$\mathbf{G}^7$	$\mathbf{C}^{maj7}$	$\mathbf{F}^{maj7}$
$\mathbf{Bm}^{7/b5}$	$\mathbf{E}^7$	$\mathbf{Am}^7$	$\mathbf{D}^7$
$\mathbf{Gm}^7$	$\mathbf{C}^7$	$\mathbf{F}^{maj7}$	$\mathbf{Bb}^{maj7}$
$\mathbf{Em}^{7/b5}$	$\mathbf{A}^7$	$\mathbf{Dm}^7$	$\mathbf{G}^7$
$\mathbf{Cm}^7$	$\mathbf{F}^7$	$\mathbf{Bb}^{maj7}$	$\mathbf{Eb}^{maj7}$
$\mathbf{Am}^{7/b5}$	$\mathbf{D}^7$	$\mathbf{Gm}^7$	$\mathbf{C}^7$
$\mathbf{Fm}^7$	$\mathbf{Bb}^7$	$\mathbf{Eb}^{maj7}$	$\mathbf{Ab}^{maj7}$
$\mathbf{Dm}^{7/b5}$	$\mathbf{G}^7$	$\mathbf{Cm}^7$	$\mathbf{F}^7$
$\mathbf{Bbm}^7$	$\mathbf{Eb}^7$	$\mathbf{Ab}^{maj7}$	$\mathbf{Db}^{maj7}$ etc.

Chapter 7 Exercises

1. Draw the circle of fifths from memory and compare it with Example 7.

2. How many sharps or flats do these keys have?
a) Ab major b) E major c) Eb minor d) G minor

3. Name the diatonic triads of the scale of Db major.

4. Try writing out the circle-of-fourths exercise till you reach the key of C major.

Chapter 8
The Harmonic Minor Scale

The minor scale, as the related key of the major scale, is formed starting from the sixth degree of that major scale *(see Chapter 7)*. It develops quite naturally by using the Aeolian church mode scale and is a minor scale in its own right (natural minor). Since the baroque age and the advent of the major-minor system there has, however, been another minor scale which is known as the **harmonic minor**.

The Introduction of a Leading Note

The character of the natural minor is more of a modal nature with chordal polyphony, which becomes noticeable primarily because of the absence of the harmonic function of the dominant *(see P 46 to 48, Examples 14 to 17)*. The diatonic chord on V, (i.e. on the dominant) of the natural minor is a minor seventh chord *(Example 1)*.

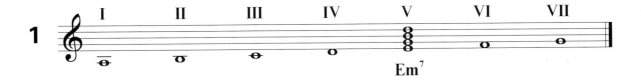

The absence of the tritone in this $\mathbf{m}^7$ chord renders it unable to create the tension necessary for a dominant function *(see P 47 ff. and Vol. II, P 10, Examples 2 and 3)*. This problem is got round by introducing an "**artificial**" **leading note** and the VIIth degree of the natural minor scale is thus raised by a half tone. **Leading notes** are defined as those which are half a tone below the note they are supposed to lead to. Through this process the diatonic chord on V becomes a dominant seventh chord *(Example 2)*.

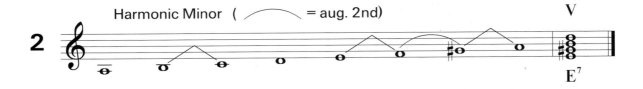

By taking a leading note from the major mode the attempt is made to endow the minor mode with more independence. As it is harmonic considerations themselves that have led to the scale being transformed, the newly formed minor scale is called the "harmonic minor".

The Dominant Seventh Chord in the Minor Cadence

Raising the 7th note of the scale logically enough means that there is also a change in the chordal structures of the harmonic minor scale in comparison with the diatonic chords of the natural minor scale *(Example 3)*.

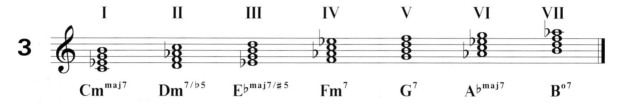

Some hitherto unknown 4-note chords materialize as diatonic seventh chords, namely Cm^{maj7}, $Eb^{maj7/\#5}$ and B^{o7}, but the most important new arrival is still the modified chord on V. The minor seventh chord in the natural minor, which cannot be put to any use as a dominant chord, becomes a dominant seventh chord by raising the 7th note of the scale. It is now possible with the diatonic chords of the harmonic minor to create the classical cadence in a minor key too, thus enabling a minor chord to form the tonic *(Example 4)*.

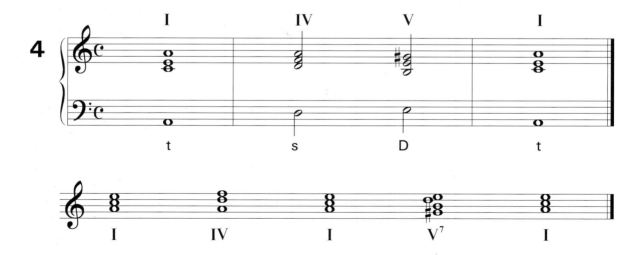

The Oriental Character of the Harmonic Minor Scale

Due to the additional minor second between the 7th and 8th note of the scale, the harmonic minor has three half-tone steps *(see Example 3)*, and as a result there is an interval of an augmented second between the 6th and 7th note of the scale, which enharmonically changed may also be regarded as a minor third. This should, however, no longer be seen as a **tonal step** (as are all seconds) but rather as a **tonal leap**, and it is this augmented tonal step (which is basically nothing short of a minor third and therefore a tonal leap) and the three half tones it encompasses - three being one more than is usually found in Western scales - that lends the harmonic minor qualities strongly reminiscent of the Orient.

The Gypsy Minor

A sound suggestive of an even more intense oriental quality can be achieved by raising the fourth degree of the harmonic minor, which corresponds to a leading note to the keynote of the dominant *(Example 5)*.

This scale now contains two augmented steps and four half-tone steps and consists - except for the whole-tone step between the 1st and 2nd note of the scale - basically of minor seconds and minor thirds only. Superimposing the notes of this scale in thirds and forming diatonic chords from them proves to be somewhat futile; this scale should be regarded more as a linear, oriental-cum-melodic structure. It is called the **zingara** or **gypsy minor** or **oriental scale** as well.

The Harmonic Minor as a Closed Scale System

Along with the Ionian system, the melodic minor system *(see Chapter 9)* and the harmonic major system *(see Chapter 11)*, the harmonic minor ranks as one of the four principle scale systems of modern harmony. Just as with the Ionian system *(see Chapter 6)*, each note of the harmonic minor is regarded as the fundamental tone or keynote of a scale in its own right. It is best to use the abbreviations Hmin 1, Hmin 2, Hmin 3 etc. to list all the diatonic scales of the harmonic minor as a complete system, the abbreviation Hmin standing for harmonic minor and the number after it indicating the degree of the scale *(Example 6)*.

6

Hmin 1 (harmonic)

Hmin 2 (Locrian ♮13)

Hmin 3 (Ionian ♯5)

Hmin 4 (Dorian ♯11)

Hmin 5 (harmonic dominant)

Hmin 6 (Lydian ♯9)

Hmin 7 (harmonic diminished)

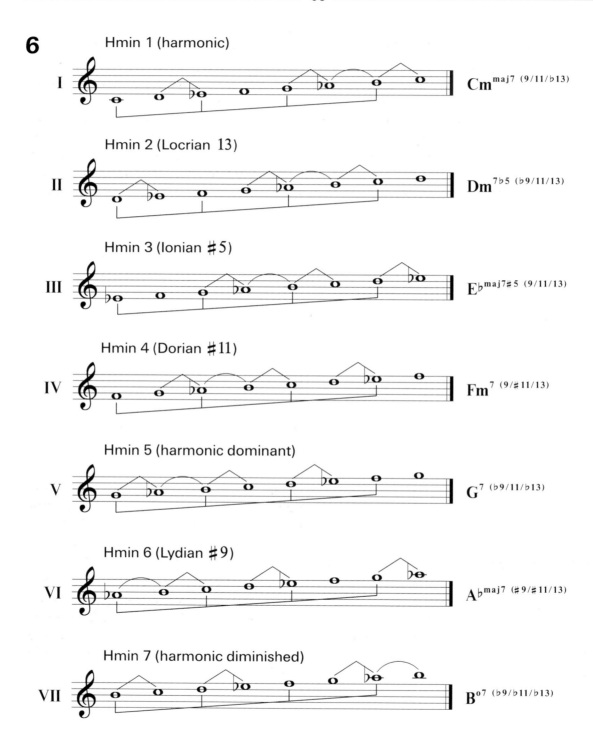

I $Cm^{maj7\ (9/11/\flat 13)}$

II $Dm^{7\flat 5\ (\flat 9/11/13)}$

III $E\flat^{maj7\sharp 5\ (9/11/13)}$

IV $Fm^{7\ (9/\sharp 11/13)}$

V $G^{7\ (\flat 9/11/\flat 13)}$

VI $A\flat^{maj7\ (\sharp 9/\sharp 11/13)}$

VII $B^{o7\ (\flat 9/\flat 11/\flat 13)}$

Naming the Diatonic Scales of the Harmonic Minor

The names of the diatonic scales of the harmonic minor have still not been standardized at an international level, the reason being that unlike, for instance, with the Ionian system, it is only in recent times that use has been made of them. This has led to the rather unsatisfactory situation of different countries and different linguistic regions having terms for the scales which are greatly at variance with each other. The best thing to do when in doubt is, then, to indicate the degree of the scale concerned in the system of the harmonic minor. You should nevertheless be able to relate the following scale names to the corresponding degrees of the harmonic minor, should you ever come across them *(Example 7).*

7

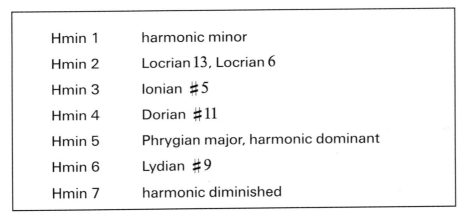

Hmin 1	harmonic minor
Hmin 2	Locrian 13, Locrian 6
Hmin 3	Ionian ♯5
Hmin 4	Dorian ♯11
Hmin 5	Phrygian major, harmonic dominant
Hmin 6	Lydian ♯9
Hmin 7	harmonic diminished

Many of these terms are in their own way logical and do make sense. Some of them follow the pattern of the scales of the Ionian system and have the name of the note that has been changed in the name of the scale (Locrian 13, Ionian ♯5, Dorian ♯11, Phrygian major, Lydian ♯9). Other terms lean more towards the chord function of the diatonic chords belonging to the scale such as "harmonic dominant" and "harmonic diminished".

There is certainly no reason why other meaningful terms cannot be found but the problem of getting them established is simply because of the lack of opportunity to disseminate such terms. It is for this very reason that I will likewise refrain from introducing this or that new term in this book. I will leave it up to the reader which names he would like to use for the scales, but when in doubt it is advisable to use the terms listed above, simply because at an international level they will generally be understood.

The Common Scales of this System

In musical practice it is mainly the scales and the chords on I, III, V and VII that are used. This is primarily because the diatonic 4-note chords on these degrees produce new sounds seen in comparison with those of the natural minor *(compare Examples 1 and 3)*. With the other degrees it is the corresponding scales of the natural minor that are preferred due to the familiarity of their sound. The scale which is by far the most important in this system is Hmin 5 (harmonic dominant) as it constitutes the primary dominant scale for minor keys and their cadences. The scales of the harmonic minor (each starting from the same keynote) on the degrees I, III, V and VII are notated as follows *(Example 8)*:

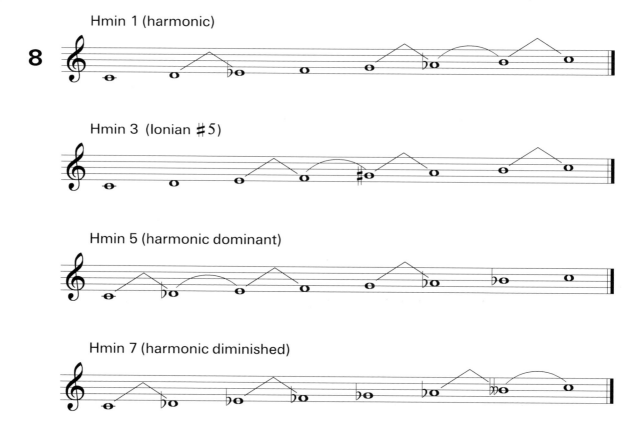

Hmin 1 (harmonic)

Hmin 3 (Ionian ♯5)

Hmin 5 (harmonic dominant)

Hmin 7 (harmonic diminished)

Harmonic Minor Half-Tone Relationships

On account of the augmented step, the scales of the harmonic minor scale system are not half-tone related to each other. There are, however, some half-tone relationships to scales of the Ionian system which are worth mentioning. The notes differing by a half tone are in brackets after the scale *(Example 9)*.

9

Hmin 1	-	Aeolian	(maj7 / 7)
Hmin 2	-	Locrian	(13 / b13)
Hmin 3	-	Ionian	(#5 / 5)
Hmin 4	-	Dorian	(#11 / 11)
Hmin 5	-	Phrygian	(3 / b3)
Hmin 6	-	Lydian	(#9 / 9)
Hmin 7	-	Mixolydian	(1 / b1)

Chapter 8 Exercises

1. What is the difference between the harmonic and the natural minor?

2. Write out the harmonic minor scale using "**d**" as the keynote.

3. Which chords previously unknown as diatonic chords are there in the harmonic minor?

4. Write out the gypsy minor scale starting on the keynote "**g**".

5. Which degree of the harmonic minor scale is the harmonic dominant scale on?

Chapter 9
The Melodic Minor Scale

In addition to the scales of the natural minor and the harmonic minor *(see Chapter 8)* there is also a third minor scale, which goes by the name of the **melodic minor**. Unlike the major mode, which knows only one major scale, the concept of the "minor scale" is not unequivocally defined. In fact it must be precisely indicated whether the minor scale is supposed to be the natural, the harmonic or the melodic minor.

Evening Out the Tonal Leap

The melodic minor scale is a further development of the harmonic minor. The leap between the 6th and 7th degrees of the harmonic minor *(see Chapter 8)*, which Western ears find unusual ("unmelodic"), is evened out by raising the 6th degree so that the upper tetrachord of the melodic minor is identical to that of the major scale *(Example 1)*. The only difference, then, between the melodic minor and the major scale is in the lower tetrachord, where a minor third establishes the minor mode.

The Melodic Minor in Classical and in Modern Music

It is because the leading note in the harmonic minor - and as a result the raising of the sixth degree in the melodic minor as well - is required only with ascending melodies, that classical harmony dispenses with raising the 6th and 7th degrees when a melody descends. This leads in classical harmony to the somewhat curious situation of the melodic minor having one structure going up and a different one coming down *(Example 2)*.

Melodic Minor ("classical")

The classical melodic minor may thus be seen as a minor scale which when ascending, is akin to the major scale (except for the minor third), and which when descending, behaves like a natural minor scale or Aeolian scale. The simultaneous presence of the natural and raised sixth and seventh degrees may have a certain charm as far as the melodic diversity is concerned, but the melodic minor in this form cannot be included in the chord-scale theory.

In modern harmony, however, the melodic minor scale is not used solely for forming melodies. Indeed, the melodic minor along with the Ionian scale, the harmonic minor scale and the harmonic major scale is looked upon as being one of the four most important scales of the chord-scale theory, with each one of the notes of this scale being considered the fundamental note of a scale in its own right. The melodic minor scale thus forms the basis of an additional chord-scale system. So as to be able to build the diatonic chords of a scale in superimposed thirds to form such a system, it is of course necessary to create a clear structure of the notes of the scale (ascending and descending), which is why the melodic minor's different make-up - depending on whether the scale is played ascending or descending - cannot be used in modern, chord-related harmony.

As the structure of the descending melodic minor is exactly the same as the notes of the natural minor, deliberations in modern harmony focus on the ascending scale with the raised degrees of VI and VII seen against the natural minor. This is why the term "melodic minor ascending" (MMA) is occasionally used to make a clear distinction. In this book the term "melodic minor" stands for the equally structured ascending and descending scale with the raised sixth and seventh degrees *(Example 3)*.

Melodic minor ("modern")

3

The Melodic Minor Scale System

In exactly the same way as it is practised with the Ionian system and the harmonic minor, it is equally possible with the melodic minor to regard each note of the scale as the keynote or tonic of a scale in its own right, which in turn can be assigned a diatonic seventh chord with its attendant options *(Example 4)*.

4

I   melodic minor   Cm^maj7 (9/11/13)

II   Dorian ♭9   Dm^7 (♭9/11/13)

III   Lydian ♯5   E♭^maj7/♯5 (9/♯11/13)

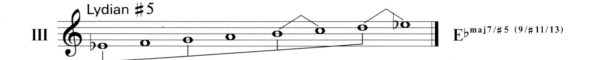

IV   Mixo ♯11   F^7 (9/♯11/13)

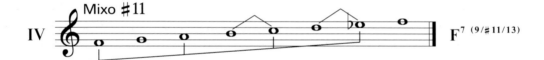

V   Mixo ♭13   G^7 (9/11/♭13)

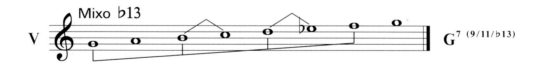

VI   Locrian 9   Am^7/♭5 (9/11/♭13)

VII   altered   B^7 (♭9/♯9/♯11/♭13)

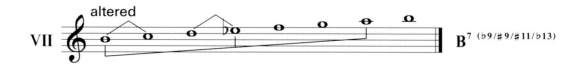

Naming the Diatonic Scales of the Melodic Minor

As is the case with the harmonic minor *(see Chapter 8)*, the terms used for the scales on each of the degrees of the melodic minor do not enjoy any broad standardization either. The multiplicity of different names for the scales is, however, even greater here due to the wider area of application of them. For this reason I would now refer you to some of the internationally most frequently used terms for these scales *(Example 5)*.

5

I	melodic minor, MMA
II	Dorian ♭9, Phrygian 13
III	Lydian ♯5, Lydian augmented
IV	Mixo ♯11, Lydian ♭7, Lydian dominant
V	Mixo ♭13
VI	Locrian 9 , Locrian ♯2, Locrian ♮2
VII	altered, super Locrian, diminished whole tone

Most of these names refer to the modified note of the relevant scale of the Ionian system, and here as well there are in some cases several options to choose from when finding a name. We should perhaps take another look at all the scales again using the same keynote, so that it is easier to see the differences between the individual scales *(Example 6)*.

6
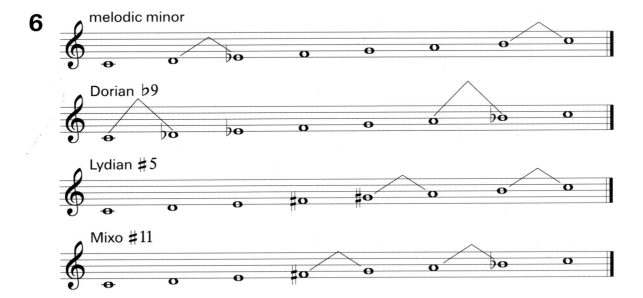

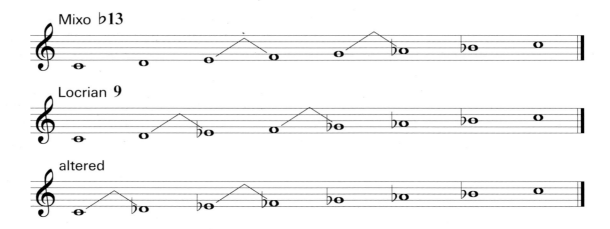

The term "Lydian augmented" refers to the augmented fifth, whilst "Lydian dominant" suggests the dominant function of this scale. We may fairly assume that the name "super Locrian" is intended to suggest that this scale, because of the lowering of the "11" - the only note not lowered with the Locrian scale - is even "more Locrian" than Locrian itself. The name "diminished whole tone" refers to the two tetrachords the altered scale is made up of. The lower tetrachord has a structure half tone - tone - half tone, which corresponds to the start of the half-tone-whole-tone scale (compare P 117, Example 24) and in American English this is also referred to as "diminished half step - whole step", while the second tetrachord is made up of whole tones only (Example 7).

Re-Interpreting the VIIth Degree

What is as such created by superimposing thirds on the VIIth degree of the melodic minor is actually a $m^{7/b5}$ seventh chord with the options b9, b11 and b13. This 4-note chord and its scale can best be illustrated by looking at the scale starting on the VIIth degree of D♭ melodic minor (Example 7).

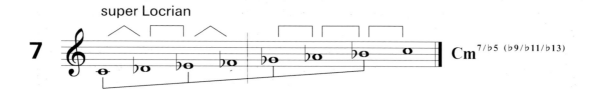

For the reasons mentioned above it makes sense to call this scale "super Locrian", and yet in the melodic minor system the diatonic chord is named as a dominant seventh chord without the fifth, having four possible optional notes *(compare Example 4)*. It is here that there has been a **re-interpretation** for certain reasons. A further scale for a $\mathbf{m}^{7/b5}$ chord is no longer required. There are already 3 scales for this 4-note chord (Locrian, Locrian 13 and Locrian 9) and they incorporate as well all the conceivable options of this chord (b9, 9, 11, b13 and 13). The only new option b11 would be classified as an avoid note anyway, so really it seems to suggest itself to "produce" a dominant scale from these notes instead.

The reason for being able to effect this re-interpretation is that on the one hand a dominant seventh chord even without the fifth is fully able to function as such, and on the other hand the scale on the **VII**th degree of the melodic minor comprises both a minor third and a major third at the same time. If we now give precedence to the major third we gain a further, urgently needed dominant scale which has four (!) frequently used options. And it doesn't end there, for these options do not appear in this combination in any other dominant scale. With all the conceivable combinations of altered optional notes it is the combination of the ♯9 with the b13 ($\mathbf{X}^{7/\sharp 9/b13}$) that must be regarded as the typical combination for the altered chord sound *(compare P 59, Example 9)*.

From Super Locrian to Altered

By changing it enharmonically *(see P 36, Example 7)* the diminished fourth (b11) of the super Locrian scale may be regarded as a major third. As a result the minor third inevitably changes to an augmented ninth (♯9) and the diminished fifth (b5) to an augmented fourth (♯11) *(Example 8)*.

altered

8    $C^{7 \ (b9/\sharp9/\sharp11/b13)}$

This scale, which is made up of the very same notes as the super Locrian scale, is called an "altered" scale. It consists of the three fundamental notes of a dominant and the four options b9, ♯9, ♯11 and b13. Due to these options this scale has the greatest dissonant content of any of the dominant scales, and the dissonance of these options may be accounted for by their being a half tone apart from the notes of a major seventh 4-note chord. The option b9 is, for instance, a half tone from the keynote, as is the option ♯9 from the major third, and this applies as well to the options ♯11 and b13 in relation to the perfect fifth *(see Volume II, Chapter 1)*.

The scale name "altered" can be traced back to the Latin "altus" (= high, low). In classical harmony the term **alteration** denotes "chromatically changed notes" and refers to those notes raised or lowered by an accidental. This then gives rise to the definition for altered chords, which says that they are chromatic changes of the chords peculiar to the scale which must resolve themselves in a half-tone step. It is generally found that notes raised by a sharp accidental tend upwards and those lowered by a flat accidental tend downwards.

It is this definition in classical harmony that gives rise to jazz harmony seeing this scale as an "altered scale". This scale, for instance, can just as easily be regarded as a dominant seventh chord (with the three elementary notes: root, major third and minor seventh), with the "altered" (chromatically changed) ninth and fifth added to it *(Example 9)*. This is a very common way of writing it in the United States today.

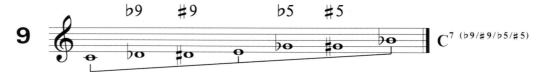

I would like at this stage to warn you against lumping together all 4-note chords with chromatically changed options such as ♭9, ♯9, ♯11, ♭13, ♭5 or ♯5 under the heading of altered chords. This may prove to be the case with many of them upon closer analysis, but altered chords in jazz harmony are meant exclusively for dominants, to which the altered scale can be played.

Melodic Minor Half-Tone Relationships

There is a multitude of scales that are half-tone related to the scales of the melodic minor system. As the melodic minor is, however, gaining increasing importance through its distinctive "modern" sound, it would seem that studying these half-tone relationships in detail would be very worthwhile. We must be mindful of the fact that just a relatively small change - after all, it is a mere one note out of seven that is raised or lowered by a half tone - produces prodigious tonal effects, which is why I would stress that this list of various half-tone relationships between scales should not lead you to assume that these scales can be interchanged at will *(Example 10)*.

10

melodic minor	-	Ionian	(♭3 / 3)
"	-	Dorian	(maj7 / 7)
"	-	Hmin 1 (harm)	(13 / ♭13)
Dorian ♭9	-	Dorian	(♭9 / 9)
"	-	Phrygian	(13 / ♭13)
"	-	Hmin 2 (Locr 13)	(5 / ♭5)
Lydian ♯5	-	Phrygian	(1 / ♯1)
"	-	Lydian	(♯5 / 5)
"	-	Hmin 3 (Ion♯5)	(♯11 / 11)
Mixo ♯11	-	Lydian	(7 / maj7)
"	-	Mixolydian	(♯11 / 11)
"	-	Hmin 4 (Dor♯11)	(3 / ♭3)
Mixo ♭13	-	Mixolydian	(♭13 / 13)
"	-	Aeolian	(3 / ♭3)
"	-	Hmin 5 (harm dom)	(9 / ♭9)
Locrian 9	-	Aeolian	(♭5 / 5)
"	-	Locrian	(9 / ♭9)
"	-	Hmin 6 (Lyd♯9)	(1 / ♭1)
altered	-	Locrian	(♭11 / 11)
"	-	Ionian	(1 / ♭1)
"	-	Hmin 7 (harm dim)	(7 / o7)

The 4 Principle Minor Keys

The frequently mind-boggling myriad of minor scales and their diatonic chords turns out to be an area of harmony of the greatest of interest, which leads me to close this chapter with an overview of the four minor scales which in their harmonic function are on the first scale degree or can be used as tonic scales.

Two of these scales find their origin in the major scale system (= Ionian system). They are the natural minor (= Aeolian) and the Dorian scale, the latter being increasingly used in this century as a tonic scale. The other two scales are the harmonic minor and the melodic minor. What is striking when comparing the notes of these scales is that the first 5 notes (!) are identical with all four, which means that the only differences between these four minor scales are to be found on the degrees VI and VII *(Example 11)*.

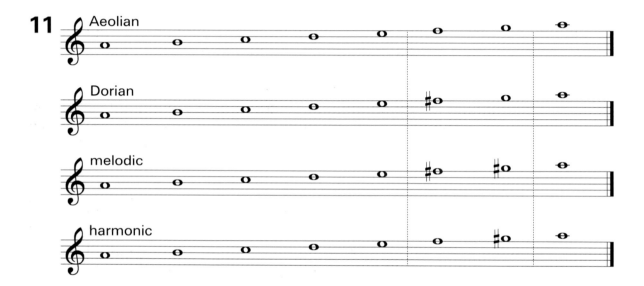

If we put all the various notes of these four scales together into one scale we get 9 different notes, and these 9 notes are exactly the same as the notes of the melodic minor scale in classical harmony *(see P 94, Example 2)*, if we include the ascending and descending notes.

We would then not be so wrong in assuming that in practice there are not really three, four or more different minor scales, but that the first five notes of the scales described above are used, and the choice of the 6th and 7th notes depends on the prevailing harmonic circumstances. This assumption is further corroborated when we consider that in classical and romantic music there is hardly a single work that is written, for instance, in the harmonic minor exclusively *(see also Vol. II, Pp 30/31)*.

It is especially interesting to look at the various diatonic seventh chords arising from these scales. They are interchangeable in virtually any way you may wish as all four scales can be used as tonic scales. We find, for instance, that a minor tonic cannot be assigned an unambiguous chord structure as a diatonic chord of the first degree.

The diatonic chord on I in a major key is either a simple major triad, a major^6 chord or a **maj7** 4-note chord (if we leave out the blues as an exception this once). All these 4-note chords use a major scale as the tonic scale.

In a minor key it is conceivable that not only a minor triad may be the diatonic chord on the first degree but also the 4-note chords $\mathbf{m}^6$, $\mathbf{m}^7$ or $\mathbf{m}^{\mathbf{maj7}}$. With a $\mathbf{m}^6$ chord both the Dorian and the melodic minor could be used as tonic scales; with $\mathbf{m}^7$ it would have to be Aeolian or Dorian, while only the harmonic or melodic minor would be possible with $\mathbf{m}^{\mathbf{maj7}}$. At first glance this does all seem to be rather complicated, yet seen within this context it is most interesting to note that a single composition may have several of these diatonic chords (and as a result their scales as well) used next to each other.

This just goes to show how complex the choice of certain diatonic chords or diatonic scales in minor keys can become. If you want to get a better general picture you can study the following table. It shows one under the other the diatonic seventh chords on all seven degrees of the four scales mentioned in the key of A minor *(Example 12)*.

12		I	II	III	IV	V	VI	VII
	Aeolian	Am^7	Bm$^{7/b5}$	C^{maj7}	Dm^7	Em^7	F^{maj7}	G^7
	Dorian	Am^7	Bm^7	C^{maj7}	D^7	Em^7	F#m$^{7/b5}$	G^{maj7}
	melodic	Am^{maj7}	Bm^7	C$^{maj7/\#5}$	D^7	E^7	F#m$^{7/b5}$	G#$^{7/alt}$
	harmonic	Am^{maj7}	Bm$^{7/b5}$	C$^{maj7/\#5}$	Dm^7	E^7	F^{maj7}	G#^{o7}

What is interesting here is that with two neighbouring scales the diatonic seventh chords of the first 6 degrees are identical on each second degree. This could be continued as well if we wrote out the diatonic seventh chords of the natural minor (Aeolian) again underneath the diatonic seventh chords of the harmonic minor. The one and only degree on which with each scale there is a diatonic chord that does not appear in any of the other three scales is the **VII** - even if we use the $\mathbf{G\#m}^{7/b5}$ formed by superimposing thirds instead of the $\mathbf{G\#}^{7/alt}$ with the melodic minor *(Example 13)*.

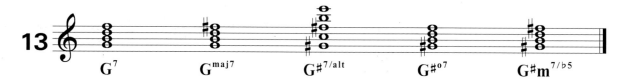

There are basically then a choice of two different diatonic seventh chords on **I** to **VI** for compositions in minor keys, while as many as five different 4-note chords may be employed on **VII**. The plain truth of the matter is then, that due to the 17 (!) possible diatonic 4-note chords, minor keys have a far greater scope for a richness in variation than major keys with their mere 7 diatonic seventh chords.

Chapter 9 Exercises

1. Write out the "classical" as well as the "modern" melodic minor scale using "**g**" as the keynote.

2. Name the diatonic 4-note chords of D melodic minor.

3. What are the following scales called?

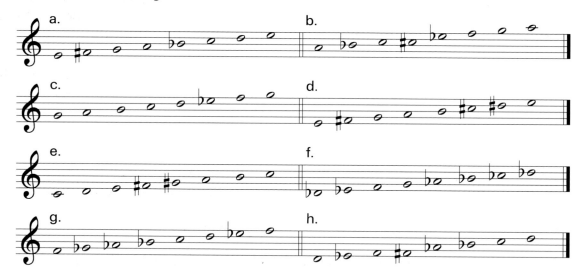

4. Which of the four principle minor keys with "**c**" as the keynote do the following diatonic 4-note chords belong to? (In some cases there may be 2 answers).

$$Dm^{7/b5}, \quad Eb^{maj7/\#5}, \quad B^{o7}, \quad Cm^{7}, \quad Am^{7/b5}, \quad F^{7}, \quad Ab^{maj7}, \quad Bb^{7} \text{ and } G^{7}.$$

Chapter 10
A General Survey of Other Scales

Apart from the scales of the four chord-scale systems Ionian, harmonic minor, melodic minor and harmonic major, there is a whole host of other scales, the most common of which I will deal with now. They are not always suitable for forming other scales and chords, and should be seen more as horizontal tone series which are suited to their own area of application or to a very special chord structure. Many of these scales have unique tonal colours and can thus be selectively employed to create special effects or to conjure up a certain mood.

1. The Pentatonic Scales

The existence of pentatonic scales can be traced back in China to the times of the Xia Dynasty (circa 1800 - 1500 B.C.), which makes them one of the oldest recorded tonal systems. The name **pentatonic** actually comes from the Greek and refers to the number of notes in this scale (Greek: pente = five).

In classical harmony the pentatonic scale is one of the four ways of dividing up the octave in the twelve-tone-tempered system, which may be illustrated as follows *(Example 1)*.

1

Pentatonic scale:	a five-note scale with 3 whole tones, 2 minor thirds and no half tones
Whole-tone scale:	a six-note scale with 6 whole tones and no half tones
Diatonic scale:	a seven-note scale with 5 whole tones and 2 half tones
Chromatic scale:	a twelve-note scale with 12 half tones

Major and Minor Pentatonic Scales

The pentatonic major scale is the result of verticalizing the intervals of 4 fifths: **c-g-d-a-e**. Placed into the same octave and arranged in order of pitch, this major pentatonic scale looks like this *(Example 2)*:

This major pentatonic scale is the only one of its kind used in classical harmony, which is why it is simply called the "pentatonic scale". But just as major scales have their relative minor scales, pentatonic scales have this major-minor relationship as well. A pentatonic scale in the minor is formed using the fifth note of the major pentatonic scale, which in general is the same as the relationship between major and minor scales, i.e. the minor scale starts a minor third lower and uses the same notes *(Example 3)*.

In principle it is in fact possible to form 5 different modes of pentatonic scales by regarding each note of the major pentatonic scale as the new fundamental tone *(Example 4)*. It is because there is no third and that therefore the mode cannot be determined that the modes 2 and 4 are seldom used. In general only the major and minor pentatonic scales are employed, i.e. the modes 1 and 5.

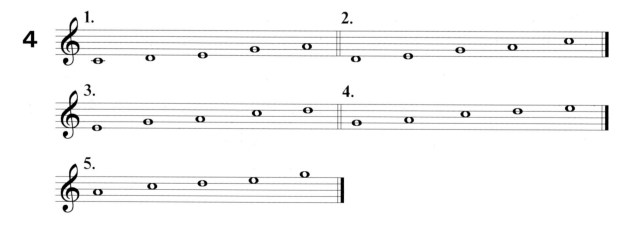

The special thing about these pentatonic scales is the absence of half-tone steps. Devoid of the tension created by the half tone and the leading note, they are largely free of functional harmonic constraints. The simplicity of their structure accounts not only for their use by virtually all the world's primitive peoples but also for their great popularity in the music of this century - and especially with styles of an improvisatory nature.

The Pentatonic Scale in Jazz

The following adjectives could generally be used to describe the tonal properties of a pentatonic scale: natural, clear, simple, transparent, consonant etc. It is especially in jazz music that these tonal qualities are used, so that despite the appearance of atonal or dissonant tonal material the connection to consonance is not lost.

The basic thinking behind the use of pentatonic scales in improvised music may be put as follows: various pentatonic scales with different keynotes can be played to the chord whose sound is meant to be improvised around. This enables the improvising musician to add various tonal colours to his playing. Logically enough, a C major pentatonic scale would go very well with a C major triad, so let's take this as an example *(Example 5)*.

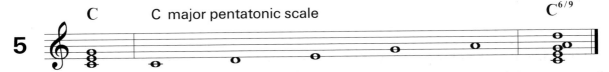

Apart from the three notes of the C major triad it has the notes **a** and **d**, which can be added to the C major triad as options. If we put the 5 notes of a major pentatonic scale together as a chord symbol we get a $C^{6/9}$ chord, which is why a 6/9 chord can be called a "**pentatonic chord**" as well. By choosing other pentatonic scales this triad can be supplemented with various other options. For instance, if we take a D major pentatonic scale the options $maj7$, 9, $\sharp 11$ and 13 are added to the C major triad *(Example 6)*.

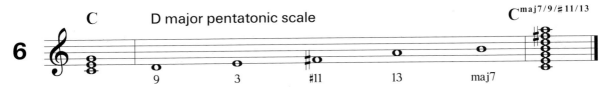

These options are the same as those in the Lydian scale *(compare Chapter 6)*. A G major pentatonic scale increases the C major triad by the options maj7, 9 and 13 *(Example 7)*, and can be used instead of a C major scale as the options of this pentatonic scale correspond to those of the Ionian scale *(see Chapter 6)*. It even has the advantage of not containing an avoid note. The absence of the fundamental tone "c" is not perceived tonally as a disadvantage. The exact opposite is in fact true, for scales not having the root of the chord do indeed sound interesting when used in improvisation.

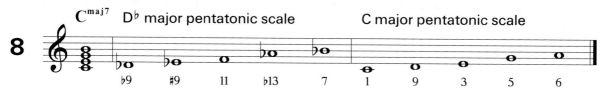

These examples can but hint at the range of possibilities available through this process, and I would recommend those of you who are interested in the subject just to listen to some triads and 4-note chords in harmony with various pentatonic major scales. You can then note down the combinations that sound interesting and use them when the harmonic circumstances allow.

Even acutely dissonant-sounding combinations of chords and pentatonic scales can, as I mentioned above, be used in the right musical context. The advantage of using the pentatonic scale to create dissonance is to be found, however, in the fact that the listener, despite the discrepancy between the notes of the underlying chord and the notes of the pentatonic scale used, can generally appreciate this form of dissonance more easily than he could just any random series of notes, this being precisely because of the clear and recognizable structure of the pentatonic scale.

The combination of a C^maj7 chord with a D♭ major pentatonic scale illustrates this rather well *(Example 8)*. The tension of this chord-scale combination can easily be resolved by the transition from the D♭ major pentatonic scale to the C major pentatonic scale a half tone lower. This example demonstrates, however, the limits of any theoretical discussion of such a process. In-depth study of such phenomena belongs to the field of jazz improvisation.

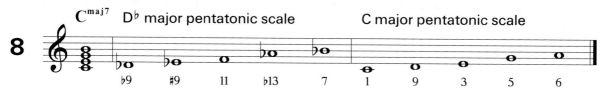

Altered Pentatonic Scales

Integrating altered pentatonic scales into harmonic theory has to be allocated to the field of jazz harmony. The basic thinking behind this is that a note of a major pentatonic scale may be altered by a half tone up or down in order to arrive at new five-tone scales. The range of alterations possible and the use of these scales is so vast that we will have to forego any attempt at precise classification and systematization. Nevertheless, there should be discussion of how this process works and I will do this by taking the most common areas of application of these altered pentatonic scales.

The preferred use of altered pentatonic scales is with dominants i.e. dominant seventh chords. In the following example there are 6 scales, which have been formed by lowering the 2nd or 5th note of the major pentatonic scale by a half tone *(Example 9)*.

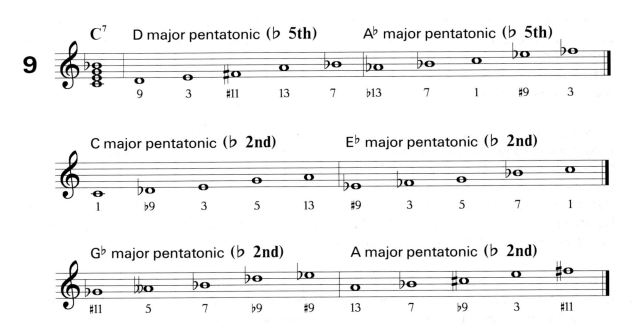

The relationship to the root of the chord C^7 can be seen below each of the notes of these scales, making it abundantly clear which options of this dominant seventh chord may be employed when using these scales in improvisation. When improvising, the musician can thus decide for him- or herself the upper structure (or the options) of the underlying 4-note chord of C^7 by choosing the individual pentatonic scale.

Indian and Japanese Pentatonic Scales

Of all the various pentatonic scales used by the peoples of this planet it is essentially those of India and Japan that have found acceptance in western harmony. They have a quite characteristic sound, which even when heard for the first time can form a link with that country. The reason for this might well be that these two scales - as opposed to what is usual with other pentatonic scales - each contain a half tone, making them especially easy to distinguish from other pentatonic scales *(Example 10)*.

2. The Scales In the Blues

The theory of harmony has traditionally had a hard time explaining the phenomenon of the blues and the scales used in this music. This can almost certainly be put down to the fact that the blues combines elements from various cultural spheres and cannot simply be explained as the result of the tradition of one culture. The one thing we can be sure of would seem to be that the blues arose from a combination of African rhythm with pentatonic melody and European harmony.

The major pentatonic scale is the only one of its kind embedded in classical European harmony, and as a result attempts are often made to trace back the scales used in blues to the major pentatonic scale or the major scale. This proves, however, to be just as inconclusive as would trying to derive the blues scales from the harmonic series.

The Minor Pentatonic Scale as the First Blues Scale

I feel the simplest way of explaining the blues and the scales used in this music is to look at what happens in practice; after all, the blues had been around for a long time before anyone got round to analyzing it. In general a simple blues played in a major key has a twelve bar form with three dominant seventh chords *(Example 11)* as the main chords, and the pentatonic minor scale formed from the keynote of the tonic is played on top of it *(Example 12)*.

11

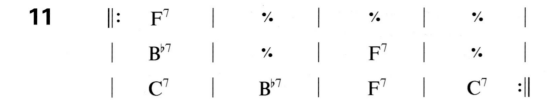

$$\|{:}\quad F^7 \quad | \quad \% \quad | \quad \% \quad | \quad \% \quad |$$
$$| \quad B^{b7} \quad | \quad \% \quad | \quad F^7 \quad | \quad \% \quad |$$
$$| \quad C^7 \quad | \quad B^{b7} \quad | \quad F^7 \quad | \quad C^7 \quad :\|$$

12

F minor pentatonic scale

The pentatonic minor scale may then be regarded as the first and simplest blues scale, and it can act as the springboard for further study and thought. What makes the blues special is the fact that on the one hand only dominant seventh chords are used as the tonic, subdominant and dominant, which is, as far as the tonic and the subdominant go, unusual and makes it a characteristic feature of the blues, and on the other hand throughout the entire form of the blues, generally but one single scale is employed as the basis for themes, melodies and improvisations. This is the second important feature of this music.

I would also mention at this point that it is precisely the blues that can be understood harmonically in many different ways. For instance, a Mixolydian scale from the root of the chord can simply be played as well to the three main chords of the blues, as is the case, for instance, with boogie-woogie. It is not so much a case of trying to analyze the blues in general; it is much more important to look at certain scales that may be used in blues (and elsewhere as well).

In order to appreciate these correlations better we should now really look at the relationships of the notes in the three blues chords of a blues in C major to the notes of the corresponding minor pentatonic scale *(Example 13)*.

13

chord	notes of the chord				C minor pentatonic scale				
					c	e^b	f	g	b^b
C^7	c	e	g	b^b	1	#9	11	5	7
F^7	f	a	c	e^b	5	7	1	9	11
G^7	g	b	d	f	11	b13	7	1	#9

What is striking is that there is not a single major third of one of the three main chords in the minor pentatonic scale. What's more, this scale has the keynote (1), the fourth (11) and the seventh (7) of each harmony. In addition to these there are the fifth (5) and the minor third ($\sharp$9) with the tonic, the fifth (5) and the ninth (9) with the subdominant, and the options$\sharp$9 and $\flat$13 with the dominant.

This example illustrates unequivocally that the blues attains its own fascination from the deliberate interplay of scales and chords, which together achieve a certain tension, and this tension is primarily found in the tonic with its semitonal friction between the major and minor third *(Example 14)*.

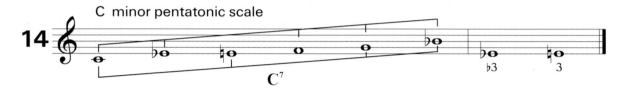

This has led some schools of harmony to regard the blues as a mixture of major and minor, which is a point of view I cannot fully endorse, particularly as blues music has been in both major and minor keys since at least the bebop era (ca. 1945 - 55). A simple blues in C minor, for instance, could go something like this *(Example 15)*:

15 $\Vert$: Cm^7 | Fm^7 | Cm^7 | ./. |

   | Fm^7 | ./. | Cm^7 | ./. |

   | Dm$^{7/\flat5}$ | G^7 | Cm^7 | G^7 :$\Vert$

The Minor Pentatonic Scale with the $\flat$5 *(Minor Blues Scale)*

The next step towards the blues scale is taken by adding the diminished fifth to the minor pentatonic scale. The minor pentatonic scale with the $\flat$5 is also called the "**minor blues scale**" or simply the "**blues scale**" *(Example 16)*.

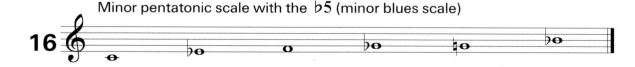

There is a predilection for using this six-tone scale on the subdominant of a blues in a major key and with the minor blues mentioned above. It is particularly in rock music that this scale has found wide favour, where it is used to create catchy melodies and **riffs**. Riffs are continually recurring (ostinato) melodies which can serve as accompanying figures as well.

The Blues Scale

The seven-note blues scale is formed by taking a minor pentatonic scale and adding the diminished fifth (as above) and the major third, which is why it is also known as the "**major blues scale**". This produces a scale with an unusual structure, which progresses chromatically from the minor third to the fifth *(Example 17)*.

Blues scale (major blues scale)

17

We cannot, however, simply go ahead and play this blues scale on top of every blues harmony. It's pretty obvious, especially with the 5 consecutive chromatic notes of the scale, that you have to exercise restraint playing one or the other note on top of the chord that is sounded, and this is palpably so with the major third of this scale, which must be adjudged an avoid note on the subdominant, as a "maj7" option cannot be played together with a dominant seventh chord *(Example 18)*.

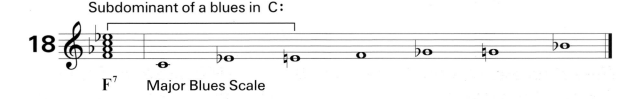

Subdominant of a blues in C:

18

F^7 Major Blues Scale

The Phenomenon of the "Blue Notes"

People are only too willing to attach the term "blue note" to chromatic auxiliary notes which cannot be explained there and then, but this term should by no means be understood as the collective name for each and every inexplicable relationship. It is in fact the words themselves (blue in the sense of "sad") that refer to the very nature of the blues and its characteristic melody.

Many attempts have been made to define the blue notes as something added on to the major scale, which is then augmented by the minor third, the diminished fifth and the minor seventh as such blue notes *(Example* 19).

What we then get is a 10-note scale which because of the excessive chromaticism cannot be used, or at best only sparingly. This does not mean to say that it is impossible when improvising to create pleasant sounding melodies using these notes: the only thing we are looking for here is a universally applicable and playable blues scale.

The truth of the matter is that blue notes should not be seen as something added to existing notes, but as notes in their own right. The minor third, for instance, should not be construed as the blue note of the major third (or vice versa), but the blue note on the third is one single note lying in pitch between the minor and the major third and actually replacing these two notes *(Example 20)*.

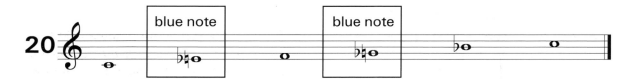

The blue note on the third is not alone, for there is a similar situation with the blue note on the fifth, which is a little lower than the fifth in our 12-tone chromatic system, and we try to get close to this pitch by adding the diminished fifth *(Example 20)*.

We can see from this that our twelve-tone chromatic system does not allow precise notation of these blue notes and this has doubtlessly contributed a great deal to their mystification. This is because of the African origin of the pentatonic blues melody, which does not fit into our European tonal system. In fact the blues scale in Example 17 originally had not seven but only five notes and is actually then a pentatonic scale. However, as there is no other viable solution at hand both thirds (the minor and the major) and both fifths (the diminished and the perfect) are played one after the other or simultaneously, and with many instruments it is also possible by bending the note and playing glissandi (by bending strings, blowing harder and more lightly, pressing down the valves only partially etc.) to get close to the pitch of these blue notes.

It is not quite the same situation with the minor seventh though, as the minor seventh used in blues can be traced back to the "natural" seventh of the harmonic series. Although it does not correspond exactly to our well-tempered minor seventh it is termed a blue note simply because its existence could not be explained in any other way. The preference for the minor seventh may have caused entirely understandable confusion in European harmony (which is strongly orientated towards functional harmony and leading notes), but strictly speaking the minor seventh in blues is not a blue note but just a simple minor seventh.

3. The Symmetrical Scales

The symmetrical scales are - as are all the other scales - divisions of an octave. Dividing the octave up into certain sections is done in this case from the aspect of symmetry, causing the sequence of half tones and/or tones to be in regular intervals.

The Whole-Tone Scale

I mentioned when describing the pentatonic scales that the whole-tone scale is likewise one of the ways of dividing up the octave in classical harmony *(see Example 1)*. As we can see from the name, the whole-tone scale consists entirely of whole tones. Altogether there are only two different whole-tone scales as they have no definite note for the beginning and the end due to the absence of half tones. Each note of a whole-tone scale can be looked upon as the tonic without the structure of the scale being changed by this. The two six-note whole-tone scales look like this *(Example 21)*:

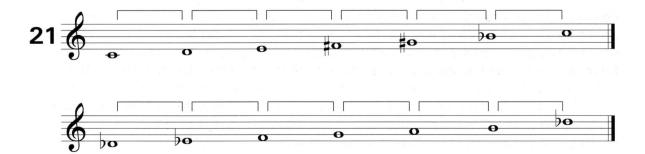

Although the whole-tone scale does not have the structure of thirds which are normally needed to form chords, it is nevertheless possible to use this scale as tonal material with certain chords. On account of the three fundamental notes of a dominant in this scale (root, major third and minor seventh) the areas of application of the whole-tone scale are manifestly limited to the dominant. It is important for the musician who is improvising to know that the notes of this scale repeat themselves at an interval of a tone. Depending on how the notes are written with accidentals there are two possible chords from this scale *(Example 22)*.

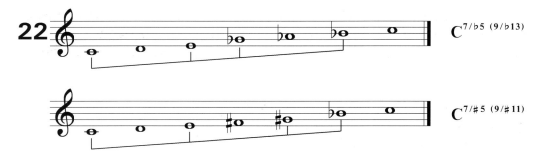

The Chromatic Scale

The chromatic scale also belongs to the four ways of dividing up the span of an octave in classical harmony *(see Example 1)*. It consists of twelve half tones, thereby containing all the 12 notes of our tonal system, and as a result it joins the whole-tone scale in having no starting or finishing point. As it has all 12 notes there is only one chromatic scale *(Example 23)* and owing to the fact that every single conceivable chord could be formed from the notes of this scale it would hardly serve any purpose assigning chords to it.

Half-Tone-Whole-Tone and Whole-Tone-Half-Tone Scales

These two scales come about by alternately putting together half tones and whole tones. Having more half tones than are usual in other scales, these scales need eight notes to fill up the range of an octave. Owing to their unusual structure and because of the number of half tones, these two scales belong to those providing the greatest tension and suspense in western harmony.

Unlike, say, the major or minor scales, these scales cannot be formed on twelve different keynotes. Due to their symmetrical structure the notes of their scales repeat themselves at an interval of a minor third, which explains why there are only three different half-tone-whole-tone and whole-tone-half-tone scales.

The Half-Tone-Whole-Tone Scale

Let's start by looking at the half-tone-whole-tone scale *(Example 24)* and we'll abbreviate its lengthy name and make it HTWT. It is also named "diminished half-whole". Despite major and minor thirds appearing simultaneously, this scale is used mainly in the dominant area.

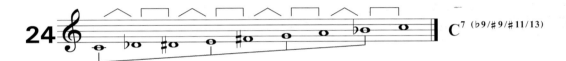

24 $C^{7\,(b9/\sharp9/\sharp11/13)}$

In some respects it is similar to the altered scale at first glance, having four optional notes, as the altered scale does, bearing strong resemblances to each other as well. Unlike altered scales, however, this half-tone-whole-tone scale has a perfect fifth. You will find a list of all the dominant scales and their options in the appendix.

Even if the area of application of this scale is more or less clearly delineated we should be mindful of the fact that this scale can go with almost any standard chord structure, enabling it to be used in improvisation as a tension-packed "universal scale". The reason for this is that a great many chords can be formed from the notes of this scale due to its symmetrical structure and its many half tones. In fact every single triad and 4-note chord shown below can be formed from the notes of HTWT *(Example 25)*.

25

C	C^6	C^7	$C^{7/b5}$
Cm	Cm^6	Cm^7	$Cm^{7/b5}$
C^o	C^{o7}		

The Whole-Tone-Half-Tone Scale

The services of the whole-tone-half-tone scale (WTHT) – also termed "diminished whole-half" – are called upon mainly to produce tension (as is the case with HTWT) though it cannot be used in as many situations as its counterpart. This may well be due to the absence of a major third *(Example 26)*. WTHT is chiefly used with the chord of C^{o7}, formed by verticalizing its thirds. It is the principle scale for diminished triads and diminished seventh chords.

Further Possibilities

Allowing the augmented step to be used as well - in addition to the half tones and whole tones used in symmetrical scales - so that further scales with a symmetrical structure can be formed, generates a range of new possibilities. Let me show you, for instance, a scale which goes under the name of the "**augmented scale**" and is occasionally used as the scale for a $maj7/\sharp5$ seventh chord *(Example 27)*. It is made up alternately of minor and augmented seconds. Due to the relatively limited situations where these scales can be used, I am not going to pursue this subject any further, but those of you who are interested in this might like to experiment by yourselves and find out how many symmetrical scales can actually be composed using minor, major and augmented seconds.

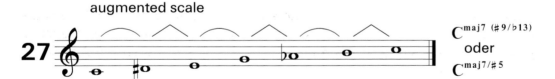

4. Composite Scales

"Composite scales" may be defined as being those that are put together according to one's individual requirements. There are no tonal holds barred here for your musical imagination and you can experiment to your heart's desire. This may come about by changing certain notes of a scale you are already familiar with or by combining this or that tetrachord, but what you should most certainly do is first to write down the notes of the chord which are to form the basis of the composite scale, and then fill in the gaps between the notes of the chord with the notes you want so that you get a scale consisting of tonal steps. Let's now look at an example.

You want to put together your own dominant scale for a dominant seventh chord with a minor ninth ($X^{7/\flat 9}$), which should resolve onto a minor tonic. The usual situation would be to use either the Hmin 5 scale or the altered scale. However, you also want the security of knowing that there are both a perfect fifth (5) and an augmented ninth ($\sharp 9$) in this scale so that you can use both of them in the chord. The combination of these two notes is not to be found in either of the two scales mentioned *(see Chapter 8 - Example 6 and Chapter 9 - Example 8)*. In order to achieve the required combination of notes it is simply a matter of combining the lower tetrachord of the altered scale with the upper tetrachord of Hmin 5 *(Example 28)*, and this leads to this composite scale being called "**harmonic altered**" *(compare Chapter 11, Example 3)*.

harmonic altered

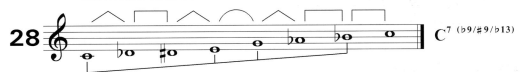

28 $C^{7\ (\flat 9/\sharp 9/\flat 13)}$

Another dominant composite scale occasionally used is produced when the major ninth of the Mixo $\sharp 11$ scale is lowered by a half tone. Logically enough, this scale is then called "Mixo $\sharp 11\flat 9$" *(see Example 29)*.

Mixo $\sharp 11\flat 9$

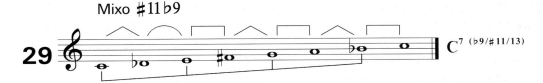

29 $C^{7\ (\flat 9/\sharp 11/13)}$

This scale can, however, just as easily be obtained from the half-tone-whole-tone scale simply by leaving out the third note of that scale. In any case care has to be exercised when using the $\sharp 9$ in the HTWT in the dominant as it is very much reminiscent of the typical altered chord sound.

After "concocting" such a composite scale you should first of all take your time to listen to it, ideally together with the chord it is to be used with. If you then find that this composite scale does actually sound convincing and you want to keep it in this form, then the only problem remaining is to find a logical and generally understandable name for it.

It is easy to see from these two examples that the "harmonyologist" is presented with truly mind-boggling potential for his concoctions, and yet the benefits of such "scaleology" do have their limits, for it is usually perfectly possible to get along quite nicely just with the scales we have studied so far. This would also seem to be the appropriate moment to remind you that as far as the harmony goes, having too many scales tends to complicate the matter rather than making it more lucid.

Chapter 10 Exercises

1. What is the difference between

    a. The harmonic and melodic minor?

    b. HTWT and altered?

    c. Mixo $\sharp 11\flat 9$ and HTWT?

    d. WTHT and Hmin 7?

2. How many half tones are there in the following scales?

    a. Dorian

    b. Melodic minor

    c. Harmonic minor

    d. Major pentatonic

    e. HTWT

    f. The major blues scale

    And which notes of the scale are these half tones between?

    [e.g. Ionian (2):   3 ⌢ 4, 7 ⌢ 8]

3. What is a "composite scale"?

4. Which scales go with the following chords?

    a. Am^{7}

    b. C^{maj7}

    c. D^{o7}

    d. $G^{7/\flat 9}$

    e. $Em^{7/\flat 5}$

    f. $A^{7/\sharp 11}$

5. What are the four principle minor scales?

6. Which other minor scales are there apart from those just mentioned?

Chapter 11
The Harmonic Major Scale

Aside from the three chord-scale systems of Ionian, melodic minor and harmonic minor, a fourth chord-scale system can be formed, its name, **the harmonic major**, being taken from its natural scale. The harmonic major scale is a major scale with the sixth note of the scale flattened, which means it can also be called "**Ionian ♭13**" *(Example 1)*.

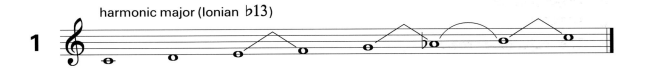

Unlike the three systems we have looked at before, the harmonic major chord-scale system is not well entrenched in musical history, but it can nevertheless be easily constructed by applying processes of logical deliberation. Such deliberation may not be entirely new[2], but as yet it has not found its place in the standard textbooks.

The Formation of the Harmonic Major Scale

The following observations may be made as regards forming the harmonic major scale: logically enough, we need a keynote as the starting point for a basic scale. The next things we need are the notes on degrees IV and V in order to be able to combine the main functions of the tonic, the subdominant and the dominant in a scale. After further deliberations we come to the conclusion that we need a leading note so that the keynote may be established as such *(compare P 87)*. We will also have to go for a major ninth (as opposed to the minor ninth), as we will otherwise very quickly hit dissonance when superimposing thirds on the chord of I. But that is not the only reason, because we will

2   "Dan Haerle: The Jazz language" Studio P/R, Miami, Florida, USA 1980; "Adelhard Roidinger: Jazz Improvisation und Pentatonic" advance music, Rottenburg/N. 1987

also need it for the fifth of the dominant chord. We now already have five of the notes of the basic scale we are constructing and in the following example with "c" as the keynote these notes are **c, d, f, g** and **b** *(Example2)*.

We now come to choosing whether it is to be the major or the minor third, which will determine the mode of the basic scale. With the sixth note of the scale we have the option of the major or the minor sixth, and if we now go through all the variations with two variable notes we find we have the following four basic scales: Ionian, melodic minor, harmonic major and harmonic minor *(see Example 5)*.

The Harmonic Major Scale System

Even the harmonic major scale lends itself to the formation of a chord-scale system, with each note of the scale being able to be seen as the keynote of a scale in its own right. This then gives rise to not only seven new scales but also to their chords - some of which are new - with the attendant options *(Example 3)*.

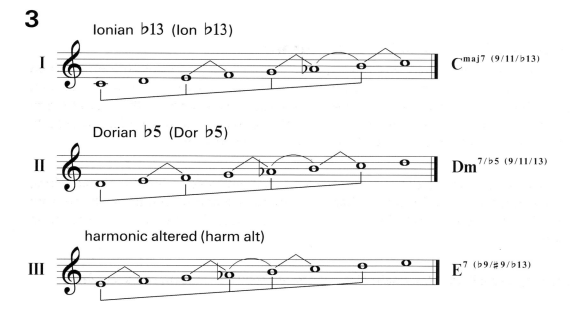

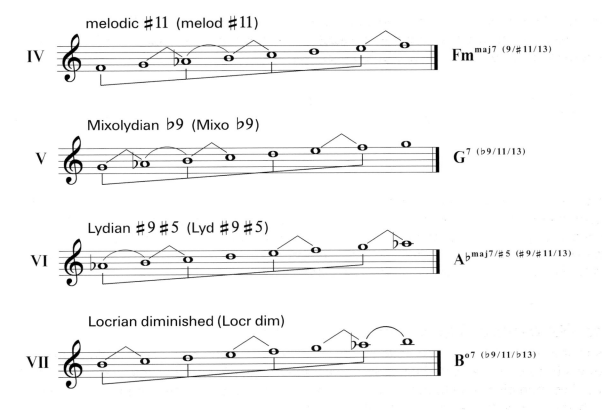

melodic #11 (melod #11)

IV   Fm$^{maj7 \ (9/\#11/13)}$

Mixolydian ♭9 (Mixo ♭9)

V   G$^{7 \ (♭9/11/13)}$

Lydian #9 #5 (Lyd #9 #5)

VI   A♭$^{maj7/\#5 \ (\#9/\#11/13)}$

Locrian diminished (Locr dim)

VII   B$^{o7 \ (♭9/11/♭13)}$

Naming the Harmonic Major Scales

Just as with the harmonic and melodic minors, there is not universal agreement as to the names of the scales of this chord-scale system, but as only few publications broach this subject there are not that many different names in any case. I have therefore tried to find as much common agreement as possible with the names we have become used to and in the other cases to use names which seem the most logical.

Another way of naming the scales is to use the system adopted for the harmonic minor, so that if we add the prefix "Hmaj" for harmonic major we can then number them from Hmaj 1 (Ionian ♭13) via Hmaj 2 (Dorian ♭5) etc. all the way through to Hmaj 7 (Locrian diminished).

The following table illustrates again all the different ways of naming these scales.

4

Hmaj 1	Ionian b13, harmonic major
Hmaj 2	Dorian b5, Locrian 9, 13
Hmaj 3	harmonic altered, altered ♮5
Hmaj 4	melodic ♯11, Lydian minor
Hmaj 5	Mixolydian b9
Hmaj 6	Lydian ♯9 ♯5, Lydian augmented ♯9
Hmaj 7	Locrian diminished

You can read up on how these scales can be used in practice in the second volume of this harmony book *(Vol. II, P 20 ff., 34/35, 49/50, 78 ff., 88/89, 136).*

The Half-Tone Relationship of the Four Basic Scales

The basic scales of the four chord-scale systems of Ionian, melodic minor, harmonic minor and harmonic major form a quartet of half-tone-related scales, with the major scale and the melodic minor sharing all the same notes of the scale, apart from the third, and thereby constituting a scale pair. It is exactly the same situation with the harmonic major and the harmonic minor, the only difference between them being the third as well. But it does not stop there: the major scale is half-tone related to the harmonic major and the melodic minor to the harmonic minor, each pair of scales having identical notes except for the major or minor sixth *(Example 5).*

5

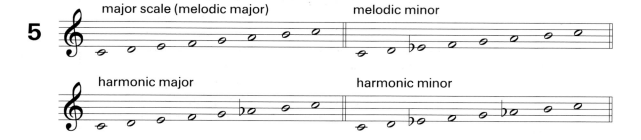

The major scale can be termed "melodic major" when listing such a four-scale system so as to underline the relationship with the melodic minor in the name of the scale as well. Naming the scales in this way produces two pairs of scales (major and minor) with the same prepositives (melodic or harmonic).

In musical practice, the half-tone relationships between scales prove to be highly useful in all kinds of improvised music when analyzing, composing and improvising. By taking some examples I would like to demonstrate which and how many half-tone relationships there are between the scales of the four chord-scale systems.

If we focus on, for instance, the scales on V of these four chord-scale systems we find the scales of Mixolydian, Mixolydian ♭13, Mixolydian ♭9 and Hmin 5 (harmonic dominant) *(Example 6)*.

6

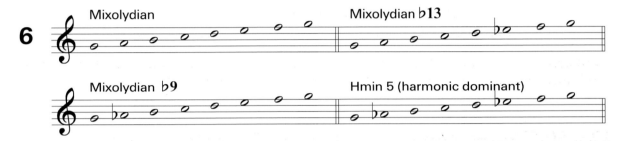

The Mixolydian scale is half-tone-related to a total of six other scales from the four chord-scale systems; Mixolydian ♭13 is related to four other scales, and Mixolydian ♭9 and Hmin 5 to three others each. These half-tone relationships can be seen in the following table *(Example 7)*.

7

Scale	half-tone-related scales	chord-scale system
Mixo	Ion, Dor Mixo ♯11, Mixo ♭13 Mixo ♭9 harm dim	Ionian melodic minor harmonic major harmonic minor
Mixo ♭13	Mixo, Aeol Ion ♭13 Hmin 5 (harm dom)	Ionian harmonic major harmonic minor
Mixo ♭9	Mixo Dor ♭9 Hmin 5 (harm dom)	Ionian melodic minor harmonic minor
Hmin 5 (harm dom)	Phryg Mixo ♭13 Mixo ♭9	Ionian melodic minor harmonic major

These half-tone relationships, which in this case concern the scales of degree V of the four chord-scale systems, can of course be applied to all seven degrees of the four systems.

In conclusion it may be said that all the scales of the Ionian system are half-tone related to a total of six scales from all four systems, and these half-tone relationships are to be found with two scales of the Ionian system, two scales of the melodic minor system and with one scale each of the harmonic major and harmonic minor systems.

All the scales of the melodic minor system are half-tone related to a total of four scales of the remaining three systems, and these relationships are to be found with two scales from the Ionian system and one scale each from the harmonic major and harmonic minor systems.

All the scales of the harmonic major and harmonic minor systems are half-tone related to a total of three scales of the remaining three systems, with the relationships being with one scale each of the other systems.

It is here that yet again the pivotal role played by the Ionian system as the basis of our western tonal system becomes abundantly apparent. The scales of the Ionian system are the only ones that are half-tone related to other scales from the same system, and as a result this gives rise to a total of six half-tone relationships to all four chord-scale systems.

The Four Chord-Scale Systems

With Ionian, melodic minor, harmonic major and harmonic minor there are four chord-scale systems comprising a total of 28 scales. Not all of these scales appear regularly in practice, but in jazz and more harmonically complex improvised music they do see the light of day, which is why it is worthwhile providing a backdrop of clarity as regards their origins and the actual differences between the individual scales. You will find all the chords belonging to the scales of the four chord-scale systems in the following table together with their options and the names of their scales *(Example 8)*.

8

	I	II	III	IV	V	VI	VII
ION	Ion maj7 9 11 13	Dor m7 9 11 13	Phryg m7 b9 11 b13	Lyd maj7 9 #11 13	Mixo 7 9 11 13	Aeol m7 9 11 b13	Locr m7/b5 b9 11 b13
MELOD	melod m^{maj7} 9 11 13	Dor b9 m7 b9 11 13	Lyd#5 maj7/#5 9 #11 13	Mixo#11 7 9 #11 13	Mixo b13 7 9 11 b13	Locr 9 m7/b5 9 11 b13	super Locr. m7/b5 b9 b11 b13
HARMON	harmon m^{maj7} 9 11 b13	Locr 13 m7/b5 b9 11 13	Ion#5 maj7/#5 9 11 13	Dor #11 m7 9 #11 13	Hmin5 7 b9 11 b13	Lyd#9 maj7 #9 #11 13	harm dim o7 b9 b11 b13
ION b13	Ion b13 maj7 9 11 b13	Dor b5 m7/b5 9 11 13	harm alt 7 b9 #9 b13	melod#11 m^{maj7} 9 #11 13	Mixo b9 7 b9 11 13	Lyd#9#5 maj7/#5 #9 #11 13	Locr dim o7 b9 11 b13
ION	Ion maj7 9 11 13	Dor m7 9 11 13	Phryg m7 b9 11 b13	Lyd maj7 9 #11 13	Mixo 7 9 11 13	Aeol m7 9 11 b13	Locr m7/b5 b9 11 b13

The sequence of the basic scales of the four scale systems is arranged in the table above in such a way that only one note changes from one scale on degree I to the next (Ionian - melodic - harmonic - Ionian b13 - Ionian). It is thus possible to see the effect caused when the note changes from degree to degree by a half tone.

For instance, if we look at degree II we see that from Dorian (Ionian degree II) to Dorian b9 (melodic minor degree II) the second note of the scale goes a half tone down. The option therefore changes from 9 to b9. From Dorian b9 (melodic minor degree II) to Locrian 13 (harmonic minor degree II) the fifth note of the scale goes a half tone down, thereby changing the chord from m^7 to m$^{7/b5}$. From Locrian 13 (harmonic minor degree II) to Dorian b5 (harmonic major degree II) the second note of the scale goes a half tone up, changing the option b9 to 9 again. And finally from Dorian b5 (harmonic major degree II) to Dorian (Ionian degree II) the fifth note of the scale again goes a half tone up, changing the chord on that degree from a m$^{7/b5}$ back to a m^7 chord.

The circle of half-tone relationships has thus gone through a full 360° and all the other degrees can also be subjected to the same procedure. The changes are of course particularly apparent when the keynote of a scale goes a half tone up or down.

Chapter 11 Exercises

1. Write out the harmonic major scale starting from the keynote "g" and the keynote "e♭".

2. Explain the difference between the scales "harmonic altered" and "altered".

3. Name the following scales.

4. Which dominant scales come from the harmonic major chord-scale system?

5. Write out all the scales in Example 7 of this chapter and study the half-tone relationships between them.

APPENDIX
Additional Chord Symbols

The symbols used to denote chords have still not been standardized at an international level. The chord symbols used in this book are geared towards those found in the United Kingdom and the USA, and they may be regarded as a standard if only for the worldwide influence of the English language and of American music. This knowledge will, however, be of limited value if you find yourself confronted with music which uses different chord symbols.

This would seem ample justification for including a list of the common chord symbols (using the chords formed on the keynote of c) which are used instead of those usually found internationally.

C^{maj7}	C^{j7}, $C^{\triangle}$, $C^{\triangle 7}$, CM^{7}, $CMaj^{7}$, CMa, CM, C_{MA}^{7}
$C^{7/\flat 9}$	$C^{7/9-}$
$C^{7/\sharp 9}$	$C^{7/9+}$
C^{7sus4}	C^{sus4}, C^{sus}, C^{4}
Cm^{7}	C^{-7}, C^{mi7}, C^{min7}, C_{MI}^{7}
$Cm^{7/\flat 5}$	$C^{-7/\flat 5}$, $C^{\emptyset 7}$, $C^{\emptyset}$
$C^{7/13}$	$C^{7/6}$
$C^{7/9/13}$	C^{13}
$C^{7/\flat 9/13}$	$C^{7/13/\flat 9}$, $C^{13/\flat 9}$
C^{o}	$C^{dim.}$
C^{o7}	$C^{dim.}$, C^{dim7}, C^{o}
C^{+}	$C^{\sharp 5}$, $C^{aug.}$, C^{5+}
$C^{7/\sharp 5}$	C^{+7}, C^{7+}, $C^{7/5+}$
C^{add9}	C^{2}
$C^{add9(no3)}$	C^{sus2}
C^{add11}	C^{4}

Tables of the Scales

The following tables of the scales are designed to provide an overview of which scales go with which chords and vice versa. These tables have been divided up into six categories, which follow the usual division of 4-note chords into five groups. The scales used in blues music have been listed separately as the sixth category due to their special harmonic individuality.

The user may gain the following information from these tables:

1. Which scales are assigned to which chord categories,

2. The names of the scales,

3. Their structure,

4. Which 4-note chord goes with them,

5. Which options can usually be added to the 4-note chords,

6. And which possible options are not generally used.

Major Scales

Name	Structure								Chord	
major penta.	1	9	3		5	13		1	major	(6/9)
Ionian	1	9	3	11	5	13	maj7	1	maj7	(9/13)
Lydian	1	9	3	♯11	5	13	maj7	1	maj7	(9/♯11/13)
Hmin 3 (Ion ♯5)	1	9	3	11	♯5	13	maj7	1	maj7/♯5	
Hmin 6 (Lyd ♯9)	1	♯9	3	♯11	5	13	maj7	1	maj7	(♯11/13)
Lydian ♯5	1	9	3	♯11	♯5	13	maj7	1	maj7/♯5	
augmented	1	♭9	3		5	♭13	maj7	1	maj7/♯5	
Ionian ♭13	1	9	3	11	5	♭13	maj7	1	maj7	(9)

Minor Scales

Name	Structure								Chord	
minor penta.	1		♭3	11	5		7	1	**m**^{7}	(11)
Aeolian	1	9	♭3	11	5	♭13	7	1	**m**^{7}	(9/11)
Dorian	1	9	♭3	11	5	13	7	1	**m**^{7}	(6/9/11)
Dorian ♭9	1	♭9	♭3	11	5	13	7	1	**m**^{7}	(6/11)
Phrygian	1	♭9	♭3	11	5	♭13	7	1	**m**^{7}	(11)
Jap. penta.	1	♭9		11	5		7	1	**m**^{7}	(11)
Hmin 4 (Dor ♯11)	1	9	♭3	♯11	5	13	7	1	**m**^{7}	(6/9)
harmonic	1	9	♭3	11	5	♭13	maj7	1	**m**^{maj7}	(9)
melodic	1	9	♭3	11	5	13	maj7	1	**m**^{maj7}	(6/9/13)
gypsy minor	1	9	♭3	♯11	5	♭13	maj7	1	**m**^{maj7}	(9)
melodic ♯11	1	9	♭3	♯11	5	13	maj7	1	**m**^{maj7}	(9/13)

Dominant Scales

Name	Structure								Chord	
major penta.	1	9	3		5	13		1	7	(9/13)
Indian penta.	1		3	11	5		7	1	7	(sus4)
Mixolyd. 1	1	9	3	11	5	13	7	1	7	(9/13)
Mixolyd. 2	1	9	3	11	5	13	7	1	7/sus4	(9/13)
Hmin 5	1	♭9	3	11	5	♭13	7	1	7	(♭9/♭13)
Mixo ♯11	1	9	3	♯11	5	13	7	1	7	(9/♯11/13)
Mixo ♯11♭9	1	♭9	3	♯11	5	13	7	1	7	(♭9/♯11/13)
Mixo ♭13	1	9	3	11	5	♭13	7	1	7	(9/♭13)
Mixo ♭9	1	♭9	3	11	5	13	7	1	7	(♭**9**/13)
whole-tone 1	1	9	3		♭5	♭13	7	1	7/♭5	(9/♭13)
whole-tone 2	1	9	3	♯11		♯5	7	1	7/♯5	(9/♯11)
harm. alt.	1	♭9	♯9	3	5	♭13	7	1	7	(♭9/♯9/♭13)
altered	1	♭9	♯9	3	♯11	♭13	7	1	7	(♭9/♯9/♭13)
HTWT	1	♭9	♯9	3	♯11 5	13	7	1	7	(♭9/♯11/13)

Half-Diminished Scales

Name	Structure								Chord	
Locrian	1	b9	b3	11	b5	b13	7	1	m7/b5	(11)
Locrian 9	1	9	b3	11	b5	b13	7	1	m7/b5	(9/11)
Hmin 2 (Locr13)	1	b9	b3	11	b5	13	7	1	m7/b5	(11)
Dorian b5	1	9	b3	11	b5	13	7	1	m7/b5	(9/11)

Diminished Scales

Name	Structure									Chord	
Hmin 7 (harm dim)	1	b9	b3	b11	b5	b13	o7		1	o7	(b13)
WTHT	1	9	b3	11	b5	b13	o7	b15	1	o7	(b13)
Locr dim	1	b9	b3	11	b5	b13	o7		1	o7	(b13)

Blues Scales

Name	Structure								Chord
blues scale	1	b3		11	b5	5	7	1	7
major blues scale	1	b3	3	11	b5	5	7	1	7

Answer Key to the Exercises

Chapter 1:

1.a. g, f, c, g, c, e, a, b, f#, b♭, c#, g♭, a♭, g#, e♭, d♭.

1.b. a, g, c, d♭, f#, e, a♭, b♭.

2. 1/1, 1/2, 1/4, 3 quarter-note/crotchet triplets = 1/2, 3/4, 1/8, 1/4.

3.a.

3.b.

4.

5.

Chapter 2:

1.

2. a. **d", f#', c', b, g#", c"'.**   b. **d, bb, Ab, c#, c', B.**

3.

a'   d   f#"   bb'   G   c   g#'   e"

Chapter 3:

1a. maj. sixth, min. tenth, maj. second, maj. seventh, min. seventh, maj. third, min. third, min. second, fourth, tritone, min. sixth, tritone.

1b. maj. third, min. seventh, min. seventh, octave, maj. sixth, min. second.

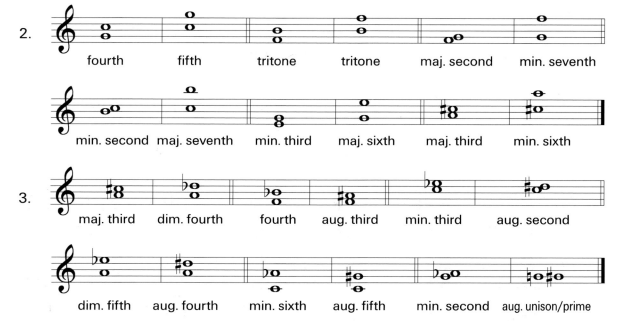

2.

fourth   fifth   tritone   tritone   maj. second   min. seventh

min. second   maj. seventh   min. third   maj. sixth   maj. third   min. sixth

3.

maj. third   dim. fourth   fourth   aug. third   min. third   aug. second

dim. fifth   aug. fourth   min. sixth   aug. fifth   min. second   aug. unison/prime

Chapter 4:

1. Fm, G⁺, A, G°, B°, E, Cm, D⁺, E♭, D♭⁺, A♭m, C#°.

2.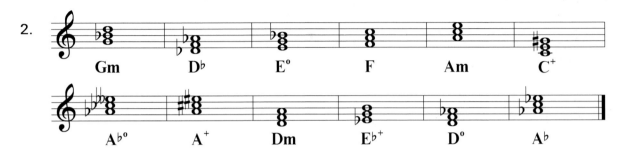

| Gm | D♭ | E° | F | Am | C⁺ |

| A♭° | A⁺ | Dm | E♭⁺ | D° | A♭ |

3. C/E, Em/G, F/A, G/D, Dm/A, Gm/B♭.

4.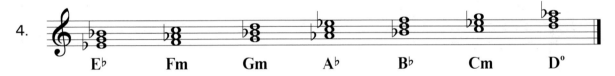

| E♭ | Fm | Gm | A♭ | B♭ | Cm | D° |

5. The scales of D major and G major have the following diatonic triads in common: D, Em, G and Bm.

Chapter 5:

1. Em⁷, F#m⁷/♭⁵, Cᵐᵃʲ⁷/#⁵, F⁶, Gm⁷, E♭ᵐᵃʲ⁷, Am⁷/♭⁵, Fm⁶, Cmᵐᵃʲ⁷, E°⁷, F⁷/ˢᵘˢ⁴, A⁷, Gmᵐᵃʲ⁷, Bm⁷, C⁶, Fᵃᵈᵈ⁹, Bm⁷/♭⁵, D⁷/#⁹/♭¹³.

2.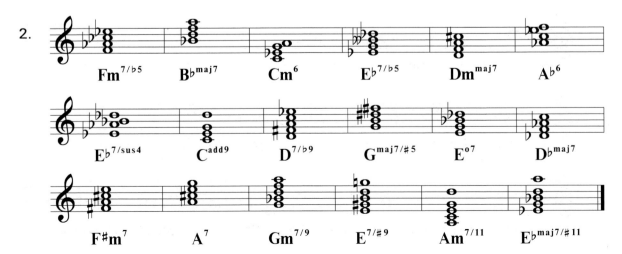

| Fm⁷/♭⁵ | B♭ᵐᵃʲ⁷ | Cm⁶ | E♭⁷/♭⁵ | Dmᵐᵃʲ⁷ | A♭⁶ |

| E♭⁷/ˢᵘˢ⁴ | Cᵃᵈᵈ⁹ | D⁷/♭⁹ | Gᵐᵃʲ⁷/#⁵ | E°⁷ | D♭ᵐᵃʲ⁷ |

| F#m⁷ | A⁷ | Gm⁷/⁹ | E⁷/#⁹ | Am⁷/¹¹ | E♭ᵐᵃʲ⁷/#¹¹ |

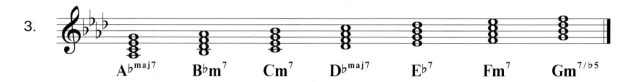

3.

| $A\flat^{maj7}$ | $B\flat m^7$ | Cm^7 | $D\flat^{maj7}$ | $E\flat^7$ | Fm^7 | $Gm^{7/\flat 5}$ |

4.   a. C^6 and Am^7.

b. $Em^{7/9}$ and $G^{maj7/13}$

c. $Em^{7/\flat 5}$ and Gm^6

d. $D^{6/9}$ and $Bm^{7/11}$

5. G/D, Dm^7, C^{add9}, Gm/D, E^7, $D^{maj7/\sharp 5}$

Chapter 6:

1.   F$\sharp$ Phrygian, E Locrian, C Mixolydian, B$\flat$ Dorian.

2.

3.   Ionian

Dorian

Phrygian

Lydian

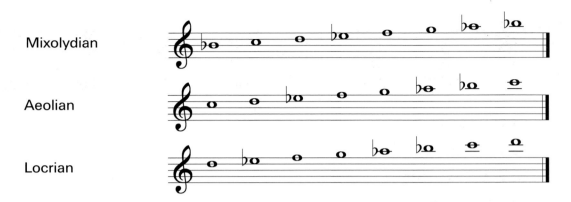

Mixolydian

Aeolian

Locrian

4. a. D Aeolian and D Mixolydian

    b. G Ionian and G♯ Locrian

Chapter 7 :

1. See the circle of fifths on Page 82.

2.

3. D♭, E♭m, Fm, G♭, A♭, B♭m, C°

4. Continuation of the circle of fourths exercise on Page 85:

. . . .				Gm$^{7/b5}$	C^7	Fm^7	B♭^{7}
E♭m^7	A♭^{7}	D♭^{maj7}	G♭^{maj7}	Cm$^{7/b5}$	F^7	B♭m^7	E♭^{7}
A♭m^7	D♭^{7}	G♭^{maj7}	C♭^{maj7}	Fm$^{7/b5}$	B♭^{7}	E♭m^7	A♭^{7}
C♯m^7	F♯^{7}	B^{maj7}	E^{maj7}	B♭m$^{7/b5}$	E♭^{7}	A♭m^7	D♭^{7}
F♯m^7	B^7	E^{maj7}	A^{maj7}	E♭m$^{7/b5}$	A♭^{7}	D♭m^7	G♭^{7}
Bm^7	E^7	A^{maj7}	D^{maj7}	G♯m$^{7/b5}$	C♯^{7}	F♯m^7	B^7
Em^7	A^7	D^{maj7}	G^{maj7}	C♯m$^{7/b5}$	F♯^{7}	Bm^7	E^7
Am^7	D^7	G^{maj7}	C^{maj7}	F♯m$^{7/b5}$	B^7	Em^7	A^7

Chapter 8:

1. In contrast to the natural minor scale, the seventh note of the harmonic minor scale is raised by a half tone/semitone.

2.

3. m^{maj7}, $maj7/\sharp5$ and $o7$.

4.

5. The harmonic dominant scale is on degree V of the harmonic minor scale.

Chapter 9:

1.

2. Dm^{maj7}, Em^7, $F^{maj7/\sharp5}$, G^7, A^7, $Bm^{7/\flat5}$, $C\sharp^{7/alt}$ (or $C\sharp m^{7/\flat5}$)

3.   a. E Locr 9   b. A alt   c. G Mixo $\flat$13   d. E melod.
       e. C Lyd $\sharp$5   f. D$\flat$ Mixo$\sharp$11   g. F Dor $\flat$9   h. D alt

4.　　**Dm**$^{7/\flat5}$　(Aeol, harm)　　**E**$\flat$**maj7/#5**　(harm, melod)

　　　B^{o7}　(harm)　　**Cm**^{7}　(Aeol, Dor)

　　　Am$^{7/\flat5}$　(Dor, melod)　　**F**^{7}　(Dor, melod)

　　　A$\flat$**maj7**　(Aeol, harm)　　**B**$\flat^7$　(Aeol)

　　　G^7　(harm, melod)

Chapter 10:

1.　a.　In contrast to the harmonic minor scale, the sixth note of the melodic minor scale is raised by a half tone/semitone. The harmonic minor scale has 3 semitone steps and the melodic minor 2.

　　b.　HTWT is a symmetrical 8-note scale. The altered scale starts on degree **VII** of melodic minor and has then only 7 notes. Unlike the altered scale, HTWT contains a perfect fifth. The only difference in the 4 options in each is that HTWT has a 13 and altered a $\flat$13.

　　c.　If the third note of the HTWT scale is taken away (the #9) we get the Mixo #11 $\flat$9 scale.

　　d.　WTHT and Hmin. 7 have the four notes of the diminished 4-note chord (^{o}7) and the sixth note of the scale in common, which means that there is a difference between the second and the fourth notes of the scale. Additionally, WTHT being an 8-note scale has one note more than Hmin. 7.

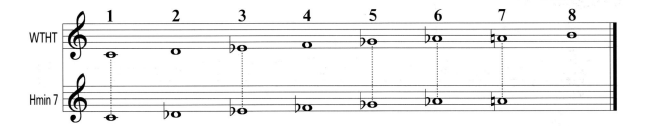

2.　a.　Dorian (2)　　　　2 ⌢ 3,　6 ⌢ 7

　　b.　melodic (2)　　　2 ⌢ 3,　7 ⌢ 8

　　c.　harmonic (3)　　2 ⌢ 3,　5 ⌢ 6, 7 ⌢ 8

　　d.　major pentatonic (0)

　　e.　HTWT (4)　　　1 ⌢ 2,　3 ⌢ 4, 5 ⌢ 6, 7 ⌢ 8

　　f.　major blues (4)　2 ⌢ 3,　3 ⌢ 4, 4 ⌢ 5, 5 ⌢ 6

3. "Composite scales" are scales that are put together according to one's individual requirements or are derived from scales already known. This generally comes about by taking away, adding or replacing a note. Another way of forming them is to combine conventional tetrachords at random.

4. a. Minor pentatonic, Dorian, Phrygian, Aeolian, Hmin. 4, Japanese pentatonic.

    b. Major pentatonic, Ionian, Lydian, Hmin. 6.

    c. WTHT, Hmin. 7

    d. Hmin. 5, HTWT, altered, Mixo ♯11 ♭9, harmonic altered.

    e. Locrian, Locrian 9, Hmin 2.

    f. Mixo ♯11, Mixo ♯11 ♭9, whole-tone, HTWT.

5. Aeolian, Dorian, harmonic minor and melodic minor.

6. Phrygian, minor pentatonic, Japanese pentatonic, gypsy minor, Hmin 4.

Chapter 11:

1.

G harmonic major   E♭ harmonic major

2. The difference between harmonic altered and altered is that the former has a perfect fifth (5) whereas the latter has a diminished fifth (♭5). As these two scales differ by this one note only, they are half-tone related to each other.

3. a. E Dor. ♭5   b. F harm. alt.   c. C♯ Locr. dim   d. C Mixo. ♭9

    e. D melod. ♯11   f. A Ion. ♭13   g. B♭ harm. alt.   h. A♭ Mixo ♭9

4. The two dominant scales of harmonic altered and Mixolydian ♭9 come from the harmonic major chord-scale system.

Index